S0-BDP-378

What people are saying about this book!

"Hopefully, all grandparents of special needs children will someday have the opportunity to read Dr. Clare Jones' wonderful new book. She provides grandparents with easy-to-understand and compassionately written descriptions of a range of childhood disabilities, along with practical, hands-on strategies for helping both their grandchildren, and their adult children, improve the quality of their lives."
—Mark Katz, Ph.D., Clinical and Consulting Psychologist and Director, Learning Development Services, San Diego, CA

"As soon as I finished reading 'Understanding Your Special Needs Grandchild' I put it in an envelope to send to my mother. With respect, tact, and sensitivity, Clare Jones guides grandparents throught the latest scientific research, and shows them how to reconcile newfangled behavioral interventions with old-fashioned parenting and moral principles. This clear and comprehensive book bridges the gap between parents struggling to raise special needs kids, and grandparents struggling to understand."
Ellen Kingsley, Editor-In-Chief, ADDitude Magazine

"This very informative resource encourages grandparents to contribute in the care of their grandchild with disabilities. It is a great way to show you positive actions to take. This is a must read for grandparents. The experienced teacher, Clare Jones, educates us about many resources, and ways to help the special needs child thrive!"
James Nahlik, Chief of Family Practice, Missouri Baptist Medical Center, St. Louis, MO

"What a wonderful resource! A sensitive, beautifully written and fascinating conversation with grandparents about their special needs grandchild. A multitude of critical information is all gathered in one very readable guide. This book is a MUST READ for any grandparent of a child with special needs—and in fact is a wonderful resource for a parent or grandparent of ANY child."
Gillian Hamilton, M.D., Ph.D.
Director, Samaritan Geriatrics Center

A Grandparents' Guide

Understanding Your
Special Needs Grandchild

Clare B. Jones, Ph.D.

Specialty Press, Inc.
300 N.W. 70th Ave., Suite 102
Plantation, Florida 33317

Copyright© 2001 Clare B. Jones

All rights reserved.

No part of this book, except those portions specifically noted, may be reproduced or transmitted in any form or by any means now known or to be invented, electronic or mechanical, including photocopying, recording, or by any information storage or retrieval system, without written permission from the author, except for brief quotations. Requests for permission or further information should be addressed to the publisher.

ISBN 1-886941-44-0

Library of Congress Cataloging-in-Publication Data
Jones, Clare B.
        Understanding your special needs grandchild: A grand-
    parents' guide / Clare B. Jones.
        p. cm.
    Includes bibliographical references and index.
    ISBN 1-886941-44-0 (alk. paper)
        1. Grandparents of handicapped children. 2. Handicapped
    children--Family relationships. 3. Handicapped
    children--Services for. 4. Grandparent and chil. I. Title.

    HQ759.9 .J66 2001
    306.874'5--dc21   00-059593

Edited by Dara Kates Levan
Cover Design by David Carlson

10 9 8 7 6 5 4 3 2 1

Printed in the United States of America

Specialty Press, Inc.
300 Northwest 70th Avenue, Suite 102
Plantation, Florida 33317
(954) 792-8100 • (800) 233-9273
www.addwarehouse.com

Dedication

This book is dedicated to the first 20 grandparents who served in the 1984 "Grandparent Read To Me Project" in Lakewood, Ohio.

And to the memory of Charlotte and Arthur Hogling and Paul and Mildred Jones, now deceased. Loving grandparents of Lindsay Jones.

Third, last year at CHADD. (Children and Adults with ...

To the Reader:

For the past 31 years I have been involved in some way with special needs children and their families. During those years I became interested in the field of gerontology and decided to do additional studies at the graduate level in this field. These studies helped me understand the families' needs and the life span of development.

The ideas for conceiving this book came from three directions. First, from the countless families who visit my practice and share their feelings about their special needs child. In reaching to serve them with their concerns and fears, I would often hear the family relate, "if only my own mother would understand about my disabled child. She never believes I am doing the right thing," and "Our parents disagree with what we are doing for our child so we avoid them and hardly talk." It was evident that some families were being divided over the care of the special needs grandchild. I observed that some of these differences were generational gaps of understanding and some were a lack of education. I wanted to write a book to help those families stay connected.

Second, in my own gerontological work and conceiving an idea for the program called *"Grandparent Read To Me"* in Lakewood, Ohio, I observed the "magic" of intergenerational relationships. I saw with my own eyes what could happen when a young child had the opportunity to work with and learn from a senior citizen and how it benefited both generations. I wanted to continue that learning experience.

Third, last year at CHADD, (Children and Adults with Attention Deficit Hyperactivity Disorder), where I am a member of the Professional Advisory Board, I was exposed to some interesting data. The number one call in the first months of the year to the CHADD hotline involved senior citizens wanting to know more about attention disorders and what happens to children with this challenge. That's when I realized the importance of writing a book for grandparents of special needs children. It was also when I recognized that perhaps the grandparent of this millennium was willing to listen to the need for change and to educate themselves to better serve their grandchildren. Thus this book, *Understanding Your Special Needs Grandchild,* was born.

In writing the book, I have attempted to cover some general ideas that grandparents could use to help their grandchildren who have special needs, regardless of the disability of their grandchild. I have also focused on a number of specific disabilities to provide more precise information on common conditions which affect children. I was only able to highlight several of these important conditions. Perhaps another volume can include many other disabilities.

As always, I thank my husband Doug, who serves as my in-house editor for all my writing efforts, and my daughter Lindsay, who now as a lawyer, shares her invaluable legal expertise.

My warmest thanks to Harvey Parker who believed in this book from the start and helped make it a reality.

Clare B. Jones, Ph.D.
Santa Fe, New Mexico
August 31, 2000

Table of Contents

Chapter One
The Circle of Life

"Grandparents need grandchildren to keep the changing world alive for them. And grandchildren need grandparents to help them know who they are and give them a sense of human experience in a world they cannot know. Here is the model of mutual learning across the generations." –Margaret Mead

The Changing Role of Grandparents

Today more than 60 million Americans are grandparents. Of that population, nearly 90 percent reportedly take an active interest in their grandchildren. Three percent of the grandparent population are currently raising one or more of their grandchildren and an additional eight percent are providing child care. By the year 2005, there will be more than 76 million grandparents in the United States. Nearly half of all grandparents at that time will be baby boomers. Currently, 50 percent of the middle-aged adults (ages 45 to 59) in the United States are grandparents. Statistics now report that nearly 5.5 million American children live with their grandparents, according to 1998 Census Bureau reports. This number has increased about 60 percent in the past two decades according to the American Association of Retired Persons.

In the homes where grandparents are the primary guardians and heading the household, 72 percent of the grandfathers and approximately 56 percent of the grandmothers work. A growing number of grandparents with 30-plus years of child rearing are now rearing their grandchildren in a new generation. Sadly, some children living with their grandparents were more likely to have a series of disadvantages. Of this population, more than one in four is

1

poor, one in three lack health insurance and more than half are on some type of public assistance. However, compared to previous generations, these grandparents are in better shape—younger, healthier, better educated—to be able to raise another generation of children compared with those grandparents who had to move in with their own kids. Today's grandparents are younger by virtue of health and lifestyle and *older* because they are living longer.

Grandparents' relationships with their grandchildren are stronger than ever. More than 10 percent of the grandparents today are caregivers for a grandchild and nearly half act as a frequent companion according to a recent study by the Applied Gerontology Group of the American Association of Retired Persons. The research revealed that 80 percent of grandparents talk on the phone with their grandchildren weekly, while 30 percent both see and talk on the phone weekly with their grandchildren. Approximately 49 percent of the grandparents interviewed for the study said they frequently act as a friend or companion to their grandchildren, and a third said they normally assume the role of adviser and confidant.

This generation of grandparents is finding the years are still golden, but they are certainly not quiet. For many people, " over 55 and a grandparent" means it's just the beginning! Today's grandparents may find themselves sharing their grandchild with another set of grandparents who are even younger than they are! The fact is that the increase in divorced and blended families may allow for some generational differences in families. Whatever the age, there is an instinctive link between grandparents. Today's grandparents are recognized for their active participation as role models with attitude and for being involved in their grandchild's life.

The role of the grandparent in the millennium erases the vision of the past –the picture of a grandparent quietly sitting in a rocking chair. Relaxation won't be a big priority for baby boomers approaching retirement. Research by Phoenix-based Del Webb Corporation indicates that many grandparents plan to continue working, taking part-time jobs and starting new careers. Of the "Boomers" 61 percent expect to work at least 20 hours per week during retirement. This survey by Webb indicated 66 percent of the baby boomers believe they will be financially more prepared for their retirement than their parents, and that they will be healthier and happier in retirement. This baby-boomer generation will impact the former profile on aging. The changes they bring about will be extraordinary. However, one thing that will remain consistent through all of these changes is the grandparent's position within the family. The function of the grandparent as a significant member of the family will remain critical in this changing world. As we enter the millennium, we see a swing to families who are recognizing the value of generational continuity. Younger families seem very keen on promoting their parents role as active grandparents. In her book, *The Essential Grandparent,* nationally known psychotherapist Dr. Lillian Carson comments, "Active grandparenting is as essential to grandparents as it is to their families. As a grandparent, you are in a unique position to make a major difference in your grandchildren's lives, and that by doing so, you will open a door to personal fulfillment and your own successful aging."

The Circle of Life

Whether you actually provide a home for your grandchildren or whether you just spend time with them, you are now beginning to experience the life process. First in this life circle, you were a child living your own childhood, and then you became a parent and experienced your child's childhood. Now you are able to observe your grandchild's. In all the excitement over having a new grandchild, don't forget that you are still a parent. Your adult children still need your support and encouragement during this new experience in their lives. The new grandchild may be the center of concentration for a while, and the new parents may feel overwhelmed with the attention. They will count on you during these times. Now is the time to do special things for your adult children to help them and also to let them know how much you care. As a new mom I will never forget when my father came to see me after the birth of my daughter, Lindsay. He arrived at the hospital with

3

two bouquets: one little one for his new granddaughter and the larger one for me, with a wonderful card saying "To Daddy's little girl, a beautiful young woman and now a mother."

One study of grandparent relationships (Cherlin & Furstenberg, 1996) found that the frequency of grandparents' contacts with their grandchildren were intimately connected to their relationship with their adult children, in particular their daughters. If you were close to your children, you will probably be close to your grandchildren.

Your involvement in your grandchild's life is primarily up to you or it may be dictated by the immediate needs of your family.

Grandparents today are often involved in new and dynamic relationships. For example, many grandparents today:

1. Are active in their grandchildren's lives after divorce. The final arrangements of the divorce often include the grandparents' visitation rights.
2. Participate in the day care and childcare roles as needed by working families.
3. Provide a significant role in financial support of the family.
4. Are the actual heads of the household where the grandchild resides.
5. Participate in intergenerational programs in schools, day care centers, and youth groups.
6. Volunteer in and are key resource people for programs addressing the disabled and infirm.

The circle of life is a framework that represents the changes that affect every family as it passes through different time periods in the life span. These changes include both developmental changes such as adolescence and nondevelopmental transition, such as divorce. This illustration demonstrates a developmental family life cycle.

The critical factor for most grandparents today is deciding what part they will play in their grandchildren's lives and how involved they want to be. The benefits of being an actively involved grandparent are multifold. These benefits can include:

1. Seeking your own personal satisfaction.
2. Strengthening family relationships.
3. Encouraging the feeling of continuum from generation to generation.
4. Taking joy in understanding that you are passing on important strategies of child rearing.
5. Taking comfort in the realization that you have been a help to your family.
6. Finding peace in knowing that you have made your mark in the circle of life.

All of the above benefits are vital and worthy. Many active grandparents have told me that becoming a grandparent was the crowning point of their family circle. Each grandchild represented a new beginning for the family. The circle of life and support is expressed beautifully in the following poem.

One Candle Power
by George Ducharme

One candle alone has the power to give light, and we empower one another by passing the flame. If we give our gift or flame to another, our flame will not be diminished, but there will be more light. The circle of support helps us ignite and inflame the desire and will in all of us to bring out the best in each other. By working together we overcome obstacles that we are unable to change by working alone. By giving our gifts, energy and our hearts to each other, we become empowered to build a future we desire. This is the gift of a circle of support.

Enter—The Grandchild!

Your unique grandchild gave you membership into this exciting world of grandparenting. Does he have "your" eyes? Do you see "your curly hair" on the tiny head in front of you? Does her laugh remind you of your own? Do you see the same facial expressions you saw on your own offspring? Your grandchild will give you membership in an entire new world of emotions, feelings and discovery. You will find yourself experiencing a potpourri of new adventures. Perhaps you may begin to have interests in new areas and feel the possibility of many new ideas! Suddenly you find yourself looking for ways to elicit giggles and smiles out of the small child before you. You may recognize a new vigor in your attitude as you hear about the child's first steps, developing vocabulary and new abilities. Many new grandparents find themselves interested again in exploring the local museums and zoological parks now that they have the delightful company of their grandchild. Your choice for a fun-packed Saturday afternoon may be that you are willing to sit through animated movies!!! You may decide that you will want to plan your vacations and days off around family events so that you can be with your grandchild. You are beginning to see the joy of sharing in a child's life and not having all the responsibility for it!

Just when you think you are enjoying this new relationship, all of sudden the balloon bursts! The phone rings and you find your-self in a conversation with your adult child about your beloved grandchild. They are calling you to tell you what they have recently learned about your grandchild, and they tell you about the child's particular challenge. In a matter of seconds you may feel as if the wind was knocked out of you. "How can this be?" you wonder. What has happened to my very wonderful grandchild?

There are certain critical dates in all our lives that mark passages of time, important life changing events and unforgettable circumstances. Do you remember where you were when President Kennedy was assassinated? Can you recall the day the Challenger Space Shuttle crashed? Just as these events place us in a certain moment in time so will the memory of the day when you learned your grandchild had a disability. You were probably momentarily stunned. No doubt your mind rushed with thoughts of just what the term or diagnosis indicated. Questions may have flooded your mind. What will happen? What will we do? What does all this mean? Perhaps you finally questioned, "How can we help?" Grandparent, your education has begun!

The family unit must pull together. It is the time to be listening to one another, to provide support and understanding. In a strong family unit, members are interrelated and experiences that affect one member affect ALL members. It is valuable for all members of the merged family to discuss the situation. As you listen to your children describe what they have found out, you recognize that both you and your grandchild are entering a new arena of life. You will begin to hear terms, services and specialties that probably were not a part of your world before. You have just joined the ranks of another group of grandparents—the *"grandparents of special needs grandchildren."* It is up to you to respond and how you respond will affect your entire family system. The circle of life moves forward. What role will you play?

How Some Families Respond to the Special Needs Child

Families vary in size, cultural identity and description. Each family is unique and so is their reaction to the needs of their special child. Each family will react differently in how they support, handle and cope with this exceptionality. In their book *Families: What makes them work*, Olson and fellow authors recognized five ways families respond to their role as caregivers of a special needs child. The five ways were:

1. <u>Passive appraisal</u>. This reaction means the family chose to ignore the problem or set it aside either temporarily or permanently, rather than working through it. In this model, the parent hopes that by ignoring it, the child will eventually catch up, "grow out of it" or cease to have the problem at all.

2. <u>Reframing</u>. In this model the family redefines the situation in an acceptable way and begins to problem solve. They purposely look at the positive side of the situation and begin to appreciate what the child contributes to the family rather than what he or she cannot do. In this model, the family identifies the child's needs, they prioritize these needs so they know what they want to work on first, and then they begin to generate workable alternatives. Once they have chosen the most appropriate course of action, they move forward with purpose and continue to evaluate their progress.

3. <u>Spiritual support</u>. In this example, the families seek spiritual guidance and support in dealing with the situation from their religious connections. They seek control and strength for the situation from the spiritual source that motivates them. Families who reach to their church, temple or another source for personal inspiration seek this direction as a means for helping them understand and accept their child.

8

4. Social support. This refers to the assistance a family gets from extended family members, friends, neighbors and co-workers. Social support can involve direct help to the child such as extending friendship to the child or including the child in activities. The social support expands the circle of life beyond the immediate family members. The child's immediate community is involved in some way in the child's life.

5. Formal support. In this last example, the family immediately seeks assistance from professionals who are trained in the specific needed area. The family will rely heavily on external support systems such as therapists, teachers and counselors. Families will look for professionals to work as a team with the family and give assistance when needed.

In considering how each family will manage, it is critical to accept that some families just adapt better than others, regardless of their challenges. It is this author's opinion that the families who have fared best and coped successfully with the special needs child are those who have used all but one of the above listed areas as a combination of resources (numbers two through five.) In some proportion, the families who have ignored or looked away from the situation (number one) eventually regretted that they had not done something sooner. The families that fare well become proactive, not reactive. They have found that developing personal accountability through natural and logical consequences has helped them respond appropriately to whatever came along. They have been able to develop relationships that stress a balance between rights and responsibilities. All children benefit when families are goal oriented, positive and willing to work with others.

Being a parent is a tough enough job today. Being a parent of a challenged child is even more difficult. Parents of disabled youth need all the support and understanding we can give.

9

Chapter Two
The Role of the "Special" Grandparent: Understanding Your Relationship

"Good family life is never an accident but always an achievement by those who share it."—James H. S. Bossard

Once you have acknowledged that you are the grandparent of a special needs grandchild, you will want to expand your perception of how you can be an active participant in your grandchild's life.

Here are five key areas that will enrich your understanding of your task as a grandparent of a special needs grandchild and empower you to be a positive role model.

1. Let go of old baggage by removing past prejudices and myths.
2. Learn about the words "unconditional love."
3. Understand what gifts you bring to this relationship.
4. Accept change readily.
5. Educate yourself about the disability.

1. Let Go of Old Baggage by Removing Past Prejudices and Myths

For many years people with disabilities were shunned and even hidden. Perhaps you remember students when you were in school ridiculed for their differences or challenges. In my own career as an educator of special needs students, I can remember when the students I taught were segregated from the other students in the school. In my very first teaching assignment, my class was given the basement classroom so other students did not have to see us during their day. Frequently the terms people have used to describe disabilities were less than kind. Terms such as " deaf and dumb," " retard," "crip" and " four eyes" still bring back horrible

11

memories for many people. Some of these terms may be part of your own vocabulary and now you must make an effort to eliminate them. In addition, you may have preconceived notions about the life of a person with a disability.

Times have changed for people with disabilities, and you must update yourself about the nature of and solution to your grandchild's condition. This is part of your grandparent education, and it is never too late to learn. It can be a painfully slow process and literally requires that you erase the old attitude and behavior. The results will be positive for you and your family. Avoid using outdated terms and read about what is happening in the particular area of disability that is now important to you. The Internet is a great resource as is the public library. A list of resources, including web sites and support organizations are listed in the resources section at the back of the book. One source of inspirational motivation is reading the autobiographies and biographies of successful disabled people. The steps many people take to overcome their handicap will inspire you.

2. Embrace What the Words "Unconditional Love" Really Mean

One day a nine-year-old boy was visiting my office and we talked for a long time about school, his interests and his family. At one point he said to me "my mom loves me but my grandpa loves ALL of me."

I responded "ALL of you—from top to bottom?" He said, "top to bottom, inside and outside!"

This boy was basking in the glow of his relationship with his grandparent knowing that no matter what he would do or think, his grandparent would still love him. He had truly experienced the term "unconditional love."

This is a phrase that describes how love will be given. It presents neither boundaries nor preconceived notions. The definition of this phrase for many denotes love, pure and simple. It describes a love that accepts a person with no limits and with no strings attached. Your love is there no matter what. When unconditional love is offered, it is easily understood, even in simple ways. The child in my office has a clear understanding of the unconditional love his grandfather gives him. This phrase is powerful, and it is an acceptance of a state of mind. Unconditional love recognizes that every child is special and in need of your love. Once recognized, there is nothing you can do or say that will change that type of love.

One adolescent client of mine was in the process of "discovering her true inner self." As part of that process, she decided to color her hair a bright fluorescent red. When her mother came home from work, she greeted her at the door and her mother went ballistic. The mother was so upset that she went in to her bedroom crying and locked the door. I have no doubt she was afraid she might do something really foolish if she stayed in the room with her daughter. About this time, the teen's grandmother visited. The teenager greeted her grandmother at the door. The grandmother did not say one word about her hair but began asking about her granddaughter's day, what's new and so forth. Finally the teenager said, "Mother is mad at me because of my hair. Did you notice I have done something with my hair?" Her grandmother wisely replied, "I did but I was so interested in you and your daily life I didn't have time to comment." The grandmother knew she had entered into a highly charged situation, and she carefully showed the grandchild she was more interested in her as a person first and foremost. The unconditional love this savvy grandmother displayed said, "I don't care what color your hair is!"

The child with a disability needs to be accepted for *who* they are, not *what* they are or what they *have*. Your acceptance of your grandchild's handicapping condition in an unconditional way will be a source of strength for your family. When you think of the challenges that face your grandchild you will want to remember this phrase: "unconditional love." Your grandchild will need to be accepted totally—and *YOU* are the right person to model this total acceptance for the family.

3. Celebrate the Very Special Person That You Are—*The Joy of You!*

One wonderful thing you bring to your grandchild is your uniqueness! Of all the grandparents in the world there is only one you! Have you ever thought about what is special about you and what you would like to pass on to your grandchild? What would you like your grandchild to learn from you?

Think about your special hobbies, interests and habits. What is unique about your personality and your life? Have you ever thought about your strengths and assets? These are treasured things that you in a very positive way can pass on to your grandchildren. Take a few minutes to think about your life and your personal life choices. Do your friends comment to you about your cheerful smile? Do you have a talent that people admire? These are the special things that separate you from another person and should be part of what you share with your grandchildren. Perhaps you collect glass paperweights? Do you enjoy fishing as a hobby? Maybe your meatloaf is what they clamor for? Do you enjoy card games and bridge? Have you become interested in the computer and consider yourself skilled in communicating in cyberspace?

Please realize that these are the extremely important things that make you exceptional in your grandchild's eyes. It is these things that you want to pass on and share with your family. This confidence in your attributes and strengths can go a long way to improving your attitude about aging. Recent studies featured in the *Journal of the American Geriatrics Society* by Harvard University professor Bekka Levy (as reported by Lauran Neergaard *Scottsdale Tribune,* November 2, 1999, pp. A6-7), suggested that the mind plays a powerful role in aging. The study found that negative attitudes and stereotypes of aging worsened people's memory and self-confidence, while positive stereotypes improved them. Positive comments help aging people change their overall mood and their self-confidence. Eventually that positive attitude impacted their behavior! So, grandparent, revel in your uniqueness and recognize the gifts you bear.

Once you recognize this area of strength, begin to provide times where you can share this with your grandchild. Perhaps you will plan a special fishing trip together where you can demonstrate your skill and teach your grandchild about fishing. Why not invite your grandchild over for dinner and involve them in the total process of the meal. Let them plan with you, cook and prepare a favorite dish. When you visit bring your cards and teach your grandchild all the bridge tricks and card games you know. For a special treat, wrap a new deck of cards for your grandchild. Take one of your favorite paperweights and gift-wrap it for your grandchild. Help start your grandchild on his or her own collection. Start e-mailing your grandchild and share favorite stories and tales of your life.

You will feel satisfaction that you are continuing a tradition or skill that can be passed from generation to generation. The Native American population, once fearing that it would lose its rich history and culture to the evolution of society, began to highlight again the importance of elders and the role they play in the family. This has resulted in many young Native Americans beginning to study the lives and traditions of their family members. Your teachings will serve to strengthen your family circle. The blessings of your life will help you weave a tapestry of memories for your grandchildren.

4. From Raggedy Ann to Barbie to Pokemon: Accepting Change

In the study of gerontology researchers have continually noted that the person who ages well is the person who can easily accept change. This includes change in their lifestyle, change in relationships and change in themselves. The process of aging is about change. The house that you saved for and lived in for many years may be replaced by a smaller home that you can now manage more easily. The friends that you cultivated and enjoyed may move or pass away leaving you to discover new friendships. The excellent health that you once had may falter. People who can accept that change is inevitable and nothing is permanent will find that they are more resilient and successful as they age. James Miller writes, "It is possible to change without growing, but it is not possible to grow without changing."

Changes also occur for your grandchildren every day. One of the most obvious changes will be observed in their culture and environment compared to what you knew as a child. Technology has thrust change into high gear, particularly in areas such as music, television, communication and computers. This change has advanced the field of special education. Many students with disabilities are now using computers, communication boards, calculators, automatic scooters, hand held spellers and electronic organizers to improve their quality of life.

The change in music has been quite radical over the generations –from Bach to Sinatra to the Bee Gees to Puff Daddy. Appreciate that your grandchildren will be interested in new things from television characters to record idols. You don't have to be an expert on pop culture to communicate with your grandchild but understanding what they are looking at, reading and listening to will make you more approachable to them.

Take time to watch new movies and television shows. Make an effort to listen to at least a few of the contemporary songs. This will help you begin to understand what is interesting to your grandchild, and these things won't seem so unusual or foreign to you. Think about what it was like when you were younger and what type of involvement you enjoyed with your grandparents. Consider when there were times you did not have the maturation to understand their needs.

Sometimes we can go too far in trying to duplicate our grandchild's interests. Several years ago a friend told me this story about her neighbor. This loving grandfather knew his grandson would be visiting and wanted to learn a little about his interests before he arrived. He found out that his grandchild really enjoyed the performer, Michael Jackson. This grandfather tuned into Michael Jackson's music and read about his lifestyle and interests.

About this time in his career Jackson was known for wearing one glove. When the grandson arrived at the airport, his grandfather was waving at him wearing one colorful sequined glove! Luckily his grandson was not easily embarrassed and took it in good stride!

Change has certainly occurred in the field of learning challenges. We have gone from shunning the handicapped individuals in our society to openly acknowledging their presence and the strengths they bring to all our lives.

This new change in your lifestyle—accepting and understanding the needs of a child—can be difficult at first but eventually will carry its own reward. The following example is the real life story of a family who learned about change through their children and their grandson who had attention-deficit/hyperactivity disorder (ADHD). It was a letter from grandparents to their children. This correspondence is an outstanding example of how grandparents can offer support to their own children when they accept the fact that perhaps their own previous thinking was wrong. Here is a living example of the anguish some families go through with the diagnosis of the child and the acceptance of it by some pretty special grandparents. The letter is reproduced here exactly as it appeared in the *Chadder (*Fall/Winter Issue, 1990), a newsletter published by Children and Adults with Attention Deficit Hyperactivity Disorder.

Dear Kids (you are still kids to us),

This letter isn't easy to write, but here goes.

A lot has happened since our grandchild was born. We remember the worry and nervousness that go along with any birth, the fear of birth defects, and the unknown...then the burst of joy when everything seems to be OK. Our expectations and hopes soared with yours, as our grandchild appeared to be free of problems and ready to thrive in this world.

We remember starting to watch you raise your child and we gave our advice generously, basing it on the wisdom we had gained from raising you...you turned out fine, which proves that we are experts!

Then, as your child grew and started to present problems that you could not solve, despite our ever-so-helpful advice, we thought to ourselves that you must have been doing something wrong. Both you, and we, his grandparents, were caught unprepared for the scenario, which began to unfold before our eyes. Behavioral patterns seen only in "other families" became a very real tragedy for you and completely misunderstood by us. We muttered in the background, "if only they would...whose genes? Not mine, for sure! Why do they indulge him? Nothing is wrong when he is with us! A good old-fashioned spanking...!"

As our advice developed an edge, we were unknowingly joining the chorus that accompanied you as you moved through your daily routines with your child. You felt blamed from all directions. People in stores glared at you as you tried, over and over, to get your child to behave. Being "obviously" bad at parenting, unable to put our infallible advice to use, constantly embarrassed you.

The next bitter pill came when you let it be known that you were seeking professional help, not only for your child, but also for yourself. To us, who had based our philosophies of life upon self-reliance and religious principles, you may as well have signed up with a witch doctor!!! We felt you were rejecting our tried-and-true ways, and were about to be exploited by false experts, who spouted mysterious labels ("oppositional," "ADD," "ADHD," "LD," fine and gross motor delay.") And other mumbo jumbo, which would take advantage of your gullibility, take your money...and does no good.

We let you know of our misgivings, but we had gotten used to your weary voices and eyes telling us, in response to our objec-

tions, what your so-called experts were telling you.

Thank God there was enough love in our family to weather those awful times, when we actually added to your burden.

And thank God you listened to the experts!

Finally, after years of heartbreak, all that mumbo jumbo started to make sense! Gradually, we began to see that our grandchild was not just a spoiled brat. We began to recognize patterns in his behavior, which were, at last, understandable to us, based upon principles promoted by your experts. We became more familiar with the jargon, as we tentatively entered what was, for us, foreign and uncharted territory.

We, who thought we were educated, experienced and tough, ARE BABES IN THE WOODS COMPARED TO YOU, you kids, who are now able to teach us.

Now we can listen to you and hear you. Although we have felt all along that we are in the same boat, now all of our oars are pulling in the same direction. It is still a rugged journey, but we hope it is a little easier now that we aren't sniping at you.

So kids, please forgive us. We hope we can heal the hurt brought about by our misunderstanding of your struggle. Our hearts are filled with love and the best of intentions for you and our grandchild. We are flesh and blood. We want so much to help that we pray that our clumsy efforts can provide some measure of comfort and support for you all!

Thanks for hanging in there, until you could reach us and teach us. One thing we have learned—you are good parents for our grandchild. The best. He needs you.

A now let us preach a little. We are lucky. We are bonded together by love, strengthened by the trials that could have fractured a less fortunate family. Thanks to that love, we have a united family support group that will not waiver, essential if our grand-child is to have a solid foundation upon which to build his life.

We will always be here for you, if you should ever need an ear, a shoulder, or, God forbid, advice. That's what grandparents are for!!!

Love, Mom and Dad

These grandparents learned to move forward in their under-standing of a disability, to put aside preconceived notions and to accept change. They admitted their lack of expertise in this area and acknowledged their children's skills in obtaining outside sup-port. These grandparents have truly embraced the meaning of the word change. You will have to be able to accept change to totally accept your special needs grandchild.

Educate Yourself About Your Grandchild's Disability

Did you think that once your reached a certain age that further education would not be a part of your life? Had you anticipated that you would no longer need to learn new information? Did you think that you could rely on your experience of years to be enough to serve you? Very few of us have the preconceived notion that as we age we want less or desire less for ourselves and our families. Chances are you have always been willing to accept that life is just a series of learning experiences. Do you agree that those who truly age well continue to seek information and knowledge? You have been given the opportunity to educate yourself in every area of this newly acquired information about your grandchild.

Move forward!

1. Read everything you can about your grandchild's disabil-ity. Be informed on what is current information and what is not. Seek opinions from a wide variety of sources knowing that you have many resources from which to choose.

2. Be aware that this is a growing process for your children as parents. Understand that to feel empowered, your children must want and seek your help, not feel as if it is being forced on them. Life is full of choices whether we make them consciously with thought and planning or whether we choose by default. The more effective our choices, the more control we have over our lives.

3. When they do seek your opinion or perhaps just seek your "listening ear," respond positively and demonstrate that you are ready to hear their concerns. Take time to be there for them and actively listen to their experiences. Avoid negative feedback such as " I told you this would happen!" or "Why didn't you do something about this immediately?" Those statements close doors and sometimes close them permanently. Hold your immediate thoughts and replace them with statements that illustrate you are listening in a very non-threatening way. Example: "I can see that you are really devoting great time to this effort" and " It is obvious that you are exploring other possibilities." *Then* offer help. " What can Mom and I do for you right now?" " Let me help out by calling the different therapists for you and get you the information to review."

This thoughtful, sensitive response and your own recently acquired knowledge will begin to help you play a pivotal and important role in your entire family's interaction. The book you are reading now will be the start of this process. Read on as you begin to gather from these pages the very education you need to be an active and positive part of your grandchild's life.

Chapter Three
Understanding Your
Grandchild's Special Needs

"Your belief in your grandchild fosters her belief in herself."—
Lillian Carson

What has brought you to this book is your love for your grandchildren and your children. Now you are also faced with the fact that your grandchild may present special challenges to your family. From the very beginning, you must choose to accept these challenges as a plus and a gift rather than a mistake. Despite their individual needs, children with disabilities bring us many blessings and the recognition that they can learn to succeed in their own way.

Open yourself to understanding this and provide unconditional love. You are being asked to give worried and overburdened parents your encouragement, support and understanding. Now is the time to become educated about the nature of the disability and begin to learn the solutions for these problems.

The Grieving Process

Raising children in today's world is difficult under any circumstances. All families face some crises in a normal life span. But when families are confronted with the real life situation of parenting a child with disabilities, family life may seem even tougher. Some families will need to go through a normal grieving process. They will need to mourn "what could have been" and begin to accept what they have. One grandfather told me, "When I heard my grandchild was blind, I felt like my dreams for that child had died. I felt like my son was given a life-long sentence of "burden."

Family members may need time to themselves, to think and perhaps to cry. These personal feelings should not be stifled because feelings must be expressed and not denied. Showing feelings openly without fear or embarrassment can help both parents and children accept the circumstances. This acceptance of feelings will be the first step to building the bridge that spans the chasm with those things in life that will make a difference—friendship, family, love, intervention and hope. Most families just need the simple gift of time to begin to regroup and prioritize their life. You can refer to the section on functional priorities for information about this.

Become Informed

The key to understanding your grandchild's disability is education. Try to become the expert resource person in this area for your family. Read all available materials, visit the library and do a search on this topic. Visit the doctor and or other professionals who specialize in this disability area and ask questions. Scan the local newspapers for information on support groups—when they meet and where. If you are familiar with the Internet, use this valuable resource to learn about national support groups and information hotlines. There is often new research listed on national web sites, and you may find some well-known experts available to you and your family this way. Reduce some of the daily burden for your children by providing them with the updated material you are able to obtain. Begin to keep a resource folder of organizations, materials and articles the family can refer to when needed.

In short, become your children's resource! This is a chance for you to make a difference in the lives of parents who may feel their lives are being overturned by the initial shock of having a child with a disability. Instead of merely offering sympathy and compassion, you have the chance to show empathy, hope and informed guidance. You can become the conduit for change. Your children will look to you with gratitude for the support you can offer. Here is your chance to make your mark and really help your loved ones. This is your opportunity to make the world a better place for your very special grandchild.

Helping your children see the special and unique qualities your grandchild brings to all of your lives will allow them to see the riches that lie within this child. As the informed grandparent, you can provide the nurturing, support and strength your children need. Then, as a team, your family can deal with this challenge effectively.

How Families Cope

Families will cope with the acknowledgment of the disability in many different ways. As we read earlier, some will choose to ignore the diagnosis, hoping it will fade away with time. Others will become very proactive and do all they can to find out about the disability. Some families will accept it as a burden and disappointment and regard everything about that difficulty as a loss. How a family reacts to and copes with the challenge depends often on the values of the family. If the family has valued each member's worth and respects each member for their right to have an opinion, they will often cope with optimism and spirit.

In the words of Dr. Thomas Lickona, researcher and author on moral development, " While we don't have a right to impose our values on our children, as parents we have the responsibility to share ours with them." Competing values within a family (i.e., several members feel differently and refuse to listen to others) create more stress for the family. Each member will be trying to work through the other members' reactions to the disability. Sometimes when several members in the family are coping well with the news, but one member is not, his/her negative resistance begins to impact all the other members. For example, I know of one family that was doing an outstanding job of managing and coping with their child's learning disability. The school had identified the problem early on, the parents sought a second opinion, and the parents were actively following a logical treatment plan. The hardest part for the family, however, was not in the day to day managing of this challenge, but rather dealing with their own parent's lack of acceptance. Their parents, the child's grandparents, continually opposed the treatment plan. They never showed any respect for the amount of time, effort and energy their children had dedicated to studying the child's disability. They never read about the treatment plan, nor did they talk to the doctors that recommended it. They chose instead to criticize everything the parents were doing. When my clients talked openly about this internal family conflict with me, they both wept. The wife said " My parents make this even more difficult—they constantly criticize us for the way we parent their grandchild saying if we would just be better parents and make our son behave we wouldn't be in this mess now." The husband said, "We find ourselves avoiding our parents now because they constantly comment negatively about our parenting skills."

This is not the first time I have heard these comments from families in my practice. I began to investigate how I could affect and influence grandparents' reactions to their special needs grandchildren. I encouraged families to bring all members to the follow-up and study sessions we held. As I worked with some grandparents, I began to notice that they did not realize the serious consequences of their actions. They did not realize that they had overlooked the important role they could have played in the lives of their grandchildren.

I also saw grandparents who had learned how to cope with the challenges their grandchild's disability brought. They were important and respected members of their family unit. In these families the grandparents stayed involved with the family members, listened and did not impose their feelings onto the family until they felt they had something to contribute. I observed first-hand the strength in those families and how beneficial their relationship was to the special needs grandchild. I learned that a supportive grandparent will find the ability to redefine a difficult situation in an acceptable way. They had many ideas to help the family solve problems.

The grandparents who were not supportive had rejected and resisted the changes the special needs child will bring to a family. They had chosen not to be involved in a positive way. These grandparents were at risk of losing a relationship with their own children and grandchildren. We all can recognize that working together as a family unit you have power. Alone by yourself, working against the family, you have nothing. The goal of this book is to help grandparents be supportive and to be involved in a positive, proactive and non-threatening way in the life of their special needs grandchild.

How To be Proactive In the Family

Look at family members' individual strengths and the strengths of the family as a unit. Use these strengths, which have helped you before, as you approach this new situation. The grandparents who are successful within special needs families have acquired the strategies of gentle appraisal. They have mastered the art of reframing their negative thoughts. They are actively participating in their family's life by using positive affirmations and respect. They have earned the right to be part of the family system, and they are valued for their contributions. They have earned this right by listening to their children, educating themselves about the disability and learning techniques that can enhance the family unit. This chapter will further explore ways to successfully be proactive in your family.

Overprotection

Parents may overprotect their children because of concern and guilt. They may offer too much help and as a result limit the child's life experiences because they are constantly fearful of what might happen. Parents and family members who smother their child may intervene too quickly and complete tasks for the child. This behavior robs the child of the many valuable life experiences.

Overprotective parents make decisions for their child and try to prevent them from the suffering negative outcomes. However, by overprotecting, parents may be hurting rather than helping their child by not giving them the opportunity and encouragement to learn on their own.

Help your children focus on what your grandchild does well, not on what he or she cannot do. Learn to recognize specific skills your grandchild exhibits and foster them. Find ways to enhance and build these skills. The recognition of strengths, rather than areas of limitation, will draw attention to the child's positive attributes. When this occurs, parents are less likely to overprotect. The best way to protect a child is to strengthen him/her so he/she can independently handle any adversity. It means teaching the child how to make effective decisions. And it means involving the child, openly discussing with the child, in a very positive manner, the child's strengths as well as challenges. This effort will result in the child seeking a way to master or cope with the challenge. Children with disabilities who openly understand their strengths and weaknesses are the children who develop control over their limitations. They become empowered to make changes and succeed.

Children with adversities who have developed into strong successful adults have developed resiliency factors. These children see problems as detours or stepping-stones in life rather than roadblocks or potholes. Survivors figure out how to resolve problems.

How can we help our grandchildren learn these skills of resiliency? We can model resiliency at an early age through our acceptance and encouragement. Show a child that he can learn from his mistakes. Encourage and help the family with making decisions and planning. Teach grandchildren ways to improve situations and creatively explore alternative situations. One way to do this is to introduce a model for building a plan or problem solving. Initially, you will have to design the plan for the child. Eventually, children can learn to do it on their own. Dr. William Glasser, a renowned therapist, has developed a way to model decision making for children, which he calls reality therapy. The following, in a brief format, is the Glasser model for teaching problem solving. The example I will use to demonstrate is that of a grandchild who has been diagnosed with a learning disability. He has some short- term memory challenges and difficulties with reading. This young boy can never remember to bring his book bag and papers back to school. There is an argument in the family every morning about trying to get him to remember the bag. The parents have taken over the responsibility for the bag, and now every morning they prepare the bag themselves and carry it into the school to avoid a daily battle. The parents are stressed with this additional responsibility, and the child is frustrated because he can sense the pressure in the family. This vicious circle is causing anger and resentment from everyone in the family. The parents have asked the grandparents to give them a brief respite by allowing the child to stay with the grandparents. The parents have also asked the grandparents for advice and help to find a solution for this difficult situation. The parents are anxious to find ways to help the child be more responsible for his book bag and papers. The following is the grandparents' plan for helping their grandchild.

Steps to Building a Plan: Teaching a Grandchild to Problem Solve

1. Be available. Demonstrate caring by listening and being a part of the child's team. Hear what the parents have to say and listen to the child's side also.
2. Determine the child's needs. What is important? *"Do you want me to help you this week while you are visiting?"*
3. Ask the child what he or she is actually doing in a noncritical way. *"What are you doing to get your homework back to school on time?"*
4. Talk to the child about evaluating his or her present behavior. *"Is getting angry with mom helping get your papers in? Would you like to do better at this?"*
5. Help design the plan. *"Let's try to put your book bag by the door every night and after two days we will talk about this."*
6. Help evaluate the plan. *"Do you think this is a good plan?"*
7. Get a commitment to the plan *"Can I count on you to put the bag there every night?"*
8. Allow the child to experience reasonable consequences.

Do not criticize or interfere with the consequences. A plan was made and if it did not work, to criticize it is to belittle the planner. Move on to design another plan.

9. Help the child evaluate follow-through. *"What did or didn't work for you? What will you do next time?"*

10. Make a copy of the plan and give it to the parents when they pick up their child. Talk openly in front of the child about the specific ways the plan worked and how the child participated in each step.

The role of the grandparent is to step back now and watch how the family continues the plan building. When the grandparent visits the family, the grandparent may continue providing input by using comments that encourage follow through. Example: *"Your Mom tells me you are remembering the plan two or three times a week now. What other ideas do you have for following through this time?"*

It is important to remember good plans take time and practice. Do not give up on teaching responsibility because you were not able to give the plan the time the child needed. Allow time for the plan to develop.

Children need the opportunity to make decisions, but they must also be accountable for their choices. They deserve respect, and they also need to learn to respect others. When children feel successful with a plan, they will find they feel more confident about themselves. Challenged children need ways to feel responsible and feel "like" other children not "unlike" them. Simple daily tasks, like learning to return and retrieve materials, help the special needs child begin to develop confidence and strength in managing his or her own life.

Your Language

When I observed families where relationships were strong and committed to one another, I noted that their verbal communication played a very important role in the relationship. They had an open communication style that allowed for comment and constructive input. However, even in the closest of family relationships, our personal comments may escape us and may endanger relationships and hurt feelings. The parent of a special needs child may feel estranged, betrayed and scared at times. These are natural feelings. However, you must never let your children feel *unvalued.* Give affirming messages to your children and help them identify specific things they are doing well. They look to you for advice, and they look to you for acceptance. Avoid criticism if you can, and if you cannot, be as sensitive as you can in expressing your thoughts.

The following verbal phrases model how to use positive, affirming language.

1. The way you handled Bobby in the store today was remarkable! You know how to quickly redirect his behavior.
2. You spend so much individual time with Matt, despite all the other demands on your time. You must feel proud of yourself for handling this so capably.
3. It took time to visit all those schools and interview the teachers. You are certainly making sure Kelly has the right school for her needs.
4. I have learned from the way you handle Justin's temper tantrums. I will try to use the exact technique if we are together and this behavior happens.
5. You have certainly become an informed advocate for our grandson.
6. You serve as a model for Andrea every day.
7. You are teaching John to be self-sufficient and independent. I am so impressed with the self- control he has now.
8. The planner you use for keeping appointments for the children is so helpful. The time you take to organize their days and appointments makes their day so successful.
9. The special quiet times you provide for Anne are just what she needs to learn control.
10. Dad and I both appreciate the way you take time to include us in the children's important activities. You are very thoughtful.

11. How lucky Jason is that you were able to find such a wonderful team of doctors to help him.
12. The time you took to find just the right therapist certainly has paid off. We can see the results every day.

Offer your children spiritual guidance and social acceptance by using the words you want to model. You are giving verbal support to your children and most of all, you are keeping the family circle of communication open.

You may also use your language to impact the everyday community about the children with disabilities. In her article "Disabilities—The Language We Use," Carol Jefferson addresses this issue. She states "People with disabilities are commonplace in our lives, and it can be our responsibility to do something special about sensitizing the general public to their uniqueness and worth by the language we use in our everyday communication. There needs to be a change in the negative attitudes about people with disabilities into positive thoughts and actions" (Jefferson, 1986, p. 5). The article also suggests some alternatives to phrases that are often used. For example, she suggests the phrase "using a wheelchair" as opposed to "wheelchair bound" and replacing the words "victim" or "afflicted" with "a child who has." She concludes, "by changing our own attitudinal barriers and using a more positive communication style, we can eliminate the myths and misconceptions about people with disabilities."

You can model these terms and phrases in your everyday life. For example, when a friend notes how "hyper" your grandchild appears, respond by saying something like "Ronnie is very enthusiastic. He is working hard to control it. I am so proud of his efforts." Your language can serve as a role model for others struggling to accept your grandchild. It gives you a great opportunity to model constructive changes in communication.

Functional Priorities

Families have a variety of responsibilities that relate to the needs of all of the family members. As the family grows and changes so will their resources. The family interaction patterns and functional priorities change with each stage of family growth.

Once a family recognizes the needs of the special child they must do the following:

a. Prioritize the child's needs
b. Determine workable alternatives
c. Select the path the family will take
d. Take action
e. Stop periodically and evaluate the situation

You can guide and coach family members to seek these constructive paths while keeping your criticism and personal doubts to yourself. Always attempt to make positive comparisons to a situation, seek ways to reframe negative thoughts and look on the positive side. Your help in showing the family how to learn problem-solving skills will alter the course of events more than your negative ridicule.

Humor

Your sense of humor is so important in helping you and those around you survive and maintain a good attitude throughout life. A person who can see some of the ordinary things of life from a humorous point of view encourages us to reconsider our rigid perceptions of ourselves and others. A common misconception about the aging adult is that they have lost their sense of humor and are discouraged and negative. Your humor can add a sense of vitality to your life. Once you learn to laugh at yourself, you will also learn to laugh with others.

Taking yourself too seriously can result in negative vibes and actually destroy your health. Dr. Norman Cousins has addressed the funny side in his wonderful books, which describe his own illness and how humor played a crucial part in his healing process. In his books *The Healing Heart* (1963) and *The Anatomy of an Illness* (1979) he describes how humor became the most effective therapeutic intervention in his illness. He explains how he actually became healthier and happier through the creations of endorphins (hormones produced by the chemical changes that result from exercise, laughter and positive emotions) in his body. He introduced humor as a critical part of his healing process and it worked!

Humor can be a wonderful way for you to personally connect with your special needs grandchild. Through humor you can encourage yourself, your family and your grandchild to relate to the challenges of life in a more relaxed and more effective way. You teach your grandchild the value of fun when you demonstrate a positive, encouraging attitude toward life.

Bumper sticker on the rear end of a passing car:

If I had known grandchildren were this much fun—I would have had them first!

Chapter Four
Understanding the Disability

"Your success and happiness lie in you. External conditions are the accidents of life."—Helen Keller

The ideas in this book will be helpful to grandparents of grandchildren with a variety of disabling conditions. However, for clarity and space requirements, I decided to emphasize and include practical information on 10 of these conditions in this chapter. These are: Attention Deficit Hyperactivity Disorder (ADHD), autism, Asperger's syndrome, cerebral palsy, Down syndrome, hearing impairments, learning disabilities, speech and language difficulties, Tourette's syndrome, and vision impairments. In addition, please look to the resource section at the end of this book for specific addresses of national organizations, support groups and web sites specializing in these conditions.

The terms "handicapped" and "disabled" are used within this book. *Handicapped* describes the consequences of a disability, whereas, *disability* refers to a particular condition, such as a loss of a limb or an eye. A person is handicapped because of his or her disability. These terms vary from state to state.

Before you read about these different disabilities, there are several important terms to understand that will be helpful to your comprehension of the information in the chapter.

Definitions

Individual Educational Plan. This is a legal document written by schools to set up an educational plan for a child in school. The I.E.P., as it is called, outlines goals and objectives for the student within the school. It provides an avenue for communication between school and parents. It is a working document that is designed to serve the student's particular learning needs.

Least Restrictive Environment. This term describes that the educational environment for a special needs student should be as similar as possible to that of typical students in the "mainstream" or regular classroom without detracting from the learning and growth of the student with a disability.

Developmental disability. This refers to a condition that originates in childhood and results in a significant handicap for the individual. Conditions such as mental retardation, cerebral palsy, attention-deficit/hyperactivity disorder and learning disabilities are examples of developmental disabilities.

Diagnostic Statistical Manual of Mental Disorders. This book is published by the American Psychiatric Association. It documents all mental health disorders and provides definitions, characteristics, and suggested treatments. The manual is revised regularly and is used by psychologists, psychiatrists and other mental health professionals to diagnose mental disorders.

Neurologically impaired or neurologically handicapped. This pertains to various conditions resulting from injury or malformation of the central nervous system.

Mainstreaming. This refers to the practice of educating challenged students in regular educational settings. The student will be taught in a regular classroom and will be provided with support services when needed.

Attention Deficit Hyperactivity Disorder (ADHD)

Lazy? Space Cadet? Day Dreamer? Hyper?

Do you remember hearing these terms when you were in school? Can you remember friends and other students who fit these categories? Chances are the children who were labeled in this way are the children who had attention deficit hyperactivity disorder (ADHD). Even though this disorder has been recognized for more than 100 years, it was officially labeled ADHD in the late 1980s.

In the past, children with characteristics of ADHD were scorned and ignored. Perhaps in your generation they were even expelled from school permanently. Ansel Adams, the famous photographer, was said to have ADHD. He was expelled in sixth grade for his hyperactivity. Years later, Adams talked about his father and his reaction to his expulsion. Mr. Adams told his son "I will never call it hyperactivity. I believe it is your internal spark, and I as your father will never let it die."

To acknowledge these issues and face them directly is part of your role as an educated grandparent. It is never too late to change past thoughts and substitute them with new ideas and direction. Your understanding of ADHD can help stop the negative messages about this population.

ADHD is a neurodevelopmental disorder that affects attention and behavior. Children and adults with this disorder are impulsive, hyperactive, and/or inattentive.

There are three types of ADHD:

1. Predominantly inattentive type
2. Predominantly hyperactive-impulsive type
3. Combined type

Conservatively, about 5 percent of the population is affected by ADHD. However, some estimates are twice that amount. ADHD is five times more likely to be found in boy as compared to girls. A child's ADHD can be mild, moderate or severe. The disorder is reported in every culture in the world. A physician, a psychologist, a diagnostic specialist or a professional who is trained in the field can make the diagnosis.

Researchers have discovered that approximately 70 percent of the children with this disorder also have a parent who has ADHD or has had symptoms of ADHD as a child or adolescent. Differences in the way neurotransmitters (brain chemicals) function in the brain are presumed play an important role in ADHD.

Children with ADHD present many challenges to their parents. As infants they are more colicky, harder to console, more apt to move frequently and take longer to settle down to sleep. As they get older they may be excessively restless, and they often respond to situations with little planning and forethought. Their impulsivity makes them risk takers who often can get into trouble because they act without thinking. Those with the inattentive type of ADHD seem to be almost lethargic and under motivated. They are day-dreamers who are forgetful in daily activities.

Children with ADHD often have trouble with organization and task completion. They will appear socially immature and have trouble making and keeping friends. Parents often report that the entire family seems to revolve around the ADHD child's demands.

Children with ADHD have their biggest challenge in school. From the time they start school they have difficulty behaving, concentrating, completing work and participating appropriately in group situations. Short-term memory deficits may be apparent. This makes it hard to remember information. Many students with ADHD have fine motor coordination difficulties, and they will prefer to print. They may have difficulty with spelling. They may get 100 percent on a spelling test Friday but will forget the words by Monday!

Students with ADHD generally require more one-to-one support and supervision. Most of these children will be taught in regular classrooms. However, approximately 40 percent of them will need to receive additional support and intervention from specially trained resource teachers. Some students with ADHD may be eligible for special education programs once they are evaluated and it is determined that they need special education or related services in school.

There are very effective treatments available for children with ADHD. A multimodal treatment plan is usually followed. One part of the treatment is to educate parents about the disorder. Books and videos tapes are available to help in this effort. A second part of the treatment may focus on parents learning behavioral strategies to cope with the child and help the child manage behavior at home.

The use of medication to manage ADHD symptoms is usually a third part of the treatment. Recent studies involving large numbers of children found that medication in combination with intensive behavioral therapy is superior to other types of treatment for ADHD. A carefully monitored medication management plan with monthly follow-up and input from teachers was more effective than intensive behavior treatment alone. Stimulant medications are often the first choice of medication to treat ADHD as they have been used for many years with great success. Some of the common stimulants used are Adderall™, Ritalin™, and Dexedrine™. A new, long-acting stimulant, Concerta™, was recently approved by the Food and Drug Administration. Preliminary studies of children taking Concerta™ indicate its effects may last up to twelve hours, making it a once-a-day medication for ADHD.

The fourth part of the treatment for ADHD involves the implementation of educational accommodations in school. Teachers of students with ADHD can benefit significantly by having these accommodations in place. These accommodations can help students learn, behave, stay focused, and be better organized. Fortunately, students with ADHD are eligible for special programs and services in school, based on their disability and its severity. They may qualify for special education services. Classroom accommodations to facilitate learning, behavior, and test performance may include untimed testing, preferential seating, close supervision, daily home notes to inform parents of progress, behavior modification programs and use of peer tutoring. The Individuals with Disabilities in Education Act (IDEA) and Section 504 of the Rehabilitation Act of 1973 support and protect children with ADHD. Further information on accommodations and laws that can help students with ADHD can be obtained through organizations such as CHADD and ADDA, which are listed in the resource chapter.

There are a number of unproven or disproven treatments for ADHD. Parents should be aware that dietary change (elimination or decrease of sugar, artificial flavorings, or colorings, etc.) does not seem to help children with ADHD. Nor have other treatments such as megavitamin therapy, chiropractic manipulation, neurofeedback or biofeedback, occupational therapy, or natural supplements and remedies been proven to be of any benefit in reducing hyperactivity or impulsivity and improving attention of those affected by ADHD.

ADHD is probably the most highly researched disorder in the field of mental health and education. It has been the subject of thousands of scientific studies over the past 50 years. Nevertheless, the National Institute of Mental Health (NIMH), universities, and other research institutions continue to provide funding for additional research. This is because ADHD is such a common disorder, which affects a significant number of people and can have serious consequences for children and adults. Scientists continue to study the effectiveness of medication in treating ADHD, methods to diagnose ADHD, the role genetics plays as a cause of this disorder, and the effects of ADHD through the life span of an individual. Pharmaceutical companies are developing new medications to treat this disorder. This research should bear fruit in the next few years.

Autism

Autism is a neurobiological condition. It is characterized by difficulty with social interaction and communication and by unusual forms of repetitive behavior.

Autism was originally diagnosed by Dr. Leo Kanner in 1943. It can co-occur with other major disabilities, such as blindness, deafness, cerebral palsy and Down syndrome. Research suggests that 40 percent of the individuals with autism are mute, thereby demonstrating little or no functional verbal communication. The diagnosis of autism has increased dramatically in the past several years. In 1978 there were 1 in 10,000 children diagnosed compared to 1999 when 1 in 500 children were diagnosed with the disorder. This diagnosis has increased 500 percent in the last 10 years. As the numbers rise, so does the speculation that autism may be caused by genetic predisposition, something environmental in nature, vaccines that children are given, or diet or nutritional deficiency. Some researchers believe that the increase in diagnosis is due to greater awareness, yet federal health officials are concerned that there is far more going on than just over diagnosis.

Autism generally appears at ages 12 to 30 months. There is a higher incidence in males with the ratio ranging from 2.5 to 4 males to one female. There is no cure for autism, however children with autism may show improvement with early intervention.

Autism can range from mild to severe. Both verbal and non-verbal communication are affected. Speech abnormalities associated with autism include a lack of vocal inflection, robotic and satirical sounding speech, echolalia (repetition of words just heard), and flat, monotone verbal expression.

Children with autism have severe problems with social interaction, making it difficult (if not entirely impossible) for some to interact appropriately with peers, friends and family members. They often exhibit repetitive and stereotypic patterns of behavior, interests and activities. These activities result in self-stimulatory movements such as hand flapping, rubbing, humming and spinning.

The autistic child may have an unusual pattern of interests. For example, the child may become over-focused on certain topics or objects (e.g., watches, types of horses, baseball cards, etc). Many autistic children will have an unusual response to sensory experiences. For example, loud noises or a light touch may be almost painful for them. They may have difficulty processing abstract concepts and seem only to understand basic, concrete information.

Approximately 75 percent of autistic children and adults are mentally retarded. However, this will vary with the severity of the disorder. Less than 5 percent of the autistic population are considered savants, as depicted in the movie *Rain Man*. Savants have limited overall skills, but extraordinary abilities in such areas as mathematics, drawing or visualization.

Typically one will see an inconsistency in their learning patterns across different subjects. The autistic child will perform better with visual, concrete academic skills and will have more difficulty with abstract and concept building skills. Reading comprehension will be affected by poor comprehension of abstract information and an aloof or distracted style. However, autistic children may be excellent readers of vocabulary words although they may not understand the meaning of what they read. Math calculation, which is concrete, visual and specific, can usually be learned, but they will have difficulty with abstract math concepts and story/

word problems. It is critical in their education to have the support of speech-language pathologists. Early intervention in language therapy programs, which are functional and integrated with real life situational language, will be vital to their learning environment.

Children with this disorder are served under federal laws including the Individuals with Disabilities Education Act (IDEA). Today most school districts offer preschool programs through high school services for autistic youth. They will be eligible for and may receive services from the school speech-language pathologist, psychologist and specially trained teachers. As they obtain stronger language skills, these children may be mainstreamed and have the opportunity to be involved in regular education programs.

Early intervention is critical. There are excellent programs in communities and school districts that provide intensive early intervention including speech and language therapy services. Surely, if the diagnosis of mental retardation is not present, the possibility of higher functioning in all areas is increased. Most families will work with a pediatrician, neurologist or psychiatrist, who is experienced in the field, and a child psychologist. Some families have employed behavioral consultants to help with ideas for managing the child in the home environment. These trained professionals teach the family supportive techniques in management and control of self-abusive and inappropriate behaviors. At times, an occupational therapist is involved to evaluate any fine motor or visual-spatial skills deficits and to provide further interventions, if necessary. Some children with autism have responded to the use of music therapy. All children with autism and their parents will benefit from a team approach of concerned professionals who regularly observe and evaluate the child's progress.

No significant research breakthroughs in autism are reported at this time. Researchers are investigating both environmental and hereditary factors to explain the causes of autism. Exploratory research in the area of secretin, the pancreatic stimulating hormone produced in the small intestine, has been non-productive. Research in the area of toxins in the gastrointestinal tract is ongoing including studies with Vitamin A and the introduction of a gluten-free diet. The resulting early identification and intervention efforts have certainly improved the prognosis. There is great interest in studying this disorder and autism treatment centers are now becoming common.

Asperger's Syndrome

This syndrome was first documented in the 1940s, but it has only come into wide recognition since 1981. This is in part due to its inclusion in the Diagnostic and Statistical Manual of Mental Disorders (DSM-IV). This is the reference manual for professionals, which is used in making the diagnosis. In this manual, Asperger's syndrome is classified as a pervasive developmental disorder. Autism is also classified as this type of disorder. A diagnosis of Asperger's syndrome can be made as early as 24 months of age.

Asperger's syndrome is a complex disorder characterized by difficulties with social interaction. Children with Asperger's syndrome often have trouble making friends and understanding nuances of social behavior. They have trouble making eye contact, holding conversations, and they often misunderstand the meaning of what others communicate through language and behavior.

Children with Asperger's syndrome also tend to be physically clumsy. In contrast to autistic children, those with Asperger's syndrome generally have normal to above average intellectual ability and fundamental speech-language skills. Difficulties are noted in significant pragmatic deficits and language processing. This means that as language becomes more abstract and interactive they will have difficulty understanding the meaning of what is being said. They may not process social cues or understand subtle social suggestions. They may have repetitive speech and behavior. They often violate social rules more out of ignorance than defiance. They appear egocentric or self-absorbed causing others to find their behavior offensive. The symptoms of the disability cause them to appear distant and detached so it is hard for others to relate to them or even empathize with their struggles.

Quick social exchanges can baffle children with Asperger's and they may appear rude or disobedient. They are literally unaware how their behavior will have an impact on others. Mental rigidity is observed, and it appears to be the result of their lack of ability to understand social interaction. Asperger's syndrome is seen as a separate and distinctly different diagnosis from autism although they may seem similar. It takes a skilled clinician working with the child and the family to denote the differences.

Children with Asperger's syndrome may also have a diagnosis of learning disability, attention deficit hyperactivity disorder, or problems with mood and anxiety. Treatments should address all these conditions.

Language intervention with a speech-language pathologist will focus on pragmatic language and the understanding of social messages and rules. A focus on the nonverbal aspects of conversation is helpful. This would involve instruction in eye contact, tone of voice, body messages, as well as hand and facial gestures. The therapist will use role-playing and encourage the child to participate in re-enacting of real life social events.

A behavioral specialist or psychologist may also be involved to support the child with coping skills. The occupational therapist can assist this child develop stronger interaction by employing and addressing sensory issues (i.e., sense of touch, smell, etc). The physical therapist may also be involved to help with overall motor functioning through the use of activities that promote gross motor coordination. Parents will also learn strategies from the different therapists to use at home. They will need to take time to teach rules of social conduct, practice and to debrief the child before they enter a new situation.

The child's pediatrician, neurologist, or psychiatrist may suggest medication to support mood swings, which are often caused by the anxiety some Asperger's children develop. They can experience frustration due to their lack of skills. Often the use of medication can help them feel less anxious and more tolerant of their differences. They generally have normal intelligence and above, therefore they will most likely be in a regular inclusive classroom setting receiving related services in language or other therapies.

We recognize that children with Asperger's can gradually learn to improve their social skills. Caretakers and therapists must emphasize the child's strengths. The prognosis of this disorder is more positive when the social skills deficits are addressed early on. Early intervention is critical to these children. Their normal intellectual ability will benefit them. In addition, their focus in highly specialized interests can be monitored and supported allowing them to become specialists in many fields. Once children with this disability are understood, plans to develop their potential can be initiated.

Cerebral Palsy

Cerebral palsy is a nonprogressive disorder that generally appears in the first year or two of life and makes it difficult to smoothly control movement or posture. It is caused by a malfunctioning of, or damage to, the brain. Cerebral palsy occurs about 1 to 3 in every 1,000 infants born. This makes it one of the most common chronic health problems in children.

Causes prior to birth or during birth include birth trauma and lack of oxygen during delivery. Other factors which may produce cerebral palsy after birth include head injuries, brain hemorrhages and brain infections. The disabling conditions that occur with cerebral palsy include perceptual and motor impairments, vision and hearing losses, convulsive disorders and problems in speech. Physical signs of cerebral palsy range from weakness and floppiness of muscles to spasticity and rigidity. The actual amount of physical disability in cases of cerebral palsy varies greatly in every individual. Some students display only minor coordination problems while others have difficulty with walking and require a cane or wheelchair.

Historically, the education of students with cerebral palsy evolved from a medical model. Most children in the past were treated in hospitals or orthopedic state institutions. Their physical needs were addressed, but we ignored their need for academic and cognitive growth. Thanks to the laws supporting public education for special needs youngsters, children with cerebral palsy were allowed access to education. The result has been that the medical community and the educational community work together in educating this child. Today most students with cerebral palsy are in regular educational programming within their local public school district.

Treatment of cerebral palsy starts with a thorough evaluation of the child's fine and gross motor development. Typically the family doctor is involved with a developmental pediatrician and a pediatric neurologist. The child with cerebral palsy is most likely to have other associated problems related to their initial diagnosis. These problems may include difficulties with intellectual functioning, vision and hearing challenges and problems associated with social and emotional growth. The child will be often be given an educational assessment to evaluate learning strengths and weaknesses. This assessment helps the medical and school team understand the learning problems caused by the physical disability and those caused by behavior reactions or other problems.

The child may work with an occupational and physical therapist to develop muscle tone, muscle strength and posture. Students with severe difficulties in speech will receive support from the speech-language pathologist. They may use a communication board as another way to develop better communication skills. A computer can be provided with adaptive techniques including more efficient techniques to input written material with limited limb use. Mobility is a key treatment issue and equipment designed to enhance independent movement includes a variety of assertive devices ranging from breath controlled electric wheel chairs that climb curbs, to the new small weight scooters. Orientation specialists will be provided by the school to determine the functional needs of the youngster. They also examine the school campus to remove any physical barriers that deny equal access to the child. The child may need adaptations to schedules, adaptive equipment and techniques to encourage independent functioning. Due to the weakened physical system they may also experience stress and fatigue more readily than others.

There is a great emphasis on transition services for older adolescents with cerebral palsy. This is a continuity of services in education or training following high school. It is the goal of transition that every child leaves the educational setting with a plan and skill for a future career.

New areas of research in the field of cerebral palsy have begun to focus on early identification and research into perinatal disorders. It is hoped that information obtained prior to birth can reduce the chances of risk for the fetus. Some of these studies will focus on a suspected maternal thyroid deficiency during pregnancy. One researcher Robert Utiger, suggests the thyroid function in all pregnant woman should be tested. Additionally the research is examining the use of Vitamin A for extremely low birth weight infants that may develop later risks for cerebral palsy.

A recent commercial featuring the actor Christopher Reeve walking unassisted may be a reality for people with motor problems caused by neurological impairment. Microprocessor chips may eventually have a significant impact on the quality of life with many of the physically disabled. We continue to be amazed by the research and technology that is now available when we study cerebral palsy. For the child today, however, we must concentrate on functional daily living plans that include least restrictive education models and accommodations within the regular classroom.

Down Syndrome and Mental Retardation

Down syndrome was first described by London physician, Langdon Down. The actual cause of the syndrome was discovered in 1959. Researchers recognized that because the syndrome was present at birth that it was linked to a cell abnormality. This was confirmed with the discovery of the extra chromosome 21. The affected person will have 47 chromosomes instead of the normal amount of chromosomes, which is 46. Down syndrome is the most common chromosomal disorder. A woman's chance of giving birth to a child with Down syndrome increases with age. The chance of having a baby with this syndrome is one in 1,250 for a 25-year-old woman, one in 378 at age 35, and one in 30 at age 45.

Mental retardation is characterized by significantly below average intellectual functioning. This is accompanied by extreme deficits in two or more of the following adaptive skill areas: communication, self-care, home living, social skills, community use or self-direction.

Children with Down syndrome have characteristic features. It was called mongolism because of a superficial facial similarity to Asians of Mongolian decent. Apart from the head and facial features, the hand is characterized by a shortened and curved little finger. Muscle tone is generally reduced and head and thyroid abnormalities are common. Cosmetic surgery is being offered to Down syndrome children at birth. Some doctors are providing the option for immediate eye surgery to "clip" the fold that is present around their eye. This "clip" gives the eye the appearance of a typical round eye and lid.

The general educational experience for children with mental retardation will focus on learning basic skills with emphasis on self-help, language and social skills. The child may be mainstreamed and will receive specialized instruction in speech and language. The latter part of secondary school will be a time of vocational preparation and job placement. The educational curriculum will focus on areas such as how to use public transportation, money management, household skills and safety. The goal will be to prepare the student for life in a home community rather than an institution. Assisted living arrangements are alternatives for Down syndrome youth when they complete their educational training. Today many communities offer sheltered workshops and community group homes and apartments for the older Down syndrome individual.

The evidence today indicates that with support students with Down syndrome can function fairly independently as adults. The severity of their syndrome naturally affects this outcome, but overall when the student had the opportunity for training and vocational skills they functioned in a higher adaptive level in community-based programs.

In 1998 the National Institute of Child Health and Development began an intensive five year study of learning ability in people with Down syndrome. The study is specifically looking at the cognitive development of individuals with Down syndrome. The findings of this study will be used to develop interventions that will improve the lives of people with the syndrome and may impact the lives of others with mental retardation, too.

Hearing Impairments

The term hearing impaired is a generic term that indicates a hearing disability, but does not indicate the type or severity. There are two main types of hearing impairment. The term *deaf* refers to people who cannot use their hearing with or without amplification. The term *hard of hearing* refers to people who can improve their hearing with the use amplification and who have some residual hearing.

One of the very first recognized and noted disabilities, hearing impairment is also one of the lowest in incidence reported today. The loss may occur before birth, during the birth process or at any time after birth. The majority of people with hearing impairments have inherited their hearing loss through either dominant or recessive genes. There are other causes of hearing loss: maternal viral infections, accidents and injuries, prolonged exposure to loud noise and illness such as meningitis and encephalitis. Since modern medical care has worked to eliminate many viral infections, the number of incidences at birth have been drastically reduced.

Hearing loss can be mild, moderate or severe. The area most affected by the hearing loss will be in the development of language. Children with hearing loss experience difficulty with the quality of their linguistic information and the actual production of speech.

Every hearing-impaired individual will be involved with an audiologist for periodic audiological testing. This testing reveals the type and extent of the loss and determines the effect on speech.

After the evaluation, the audiologist can prescribe an appropriate amplification device, if necessary. Medical evaluation of the ears' function is the exclusive role of the highly trained doctors called the otologist and the otolaryngologist. They will determine if medication is necessary and if surgical intervention is appropriate. Today there are state-of-the art implants and artificially built inner ear components, which may be helpful for some types of hearing losses. Speech-language pathologists will be involved to teach speech reading (reading the face for signs and interpretations of language) and to teach pronunciation and articulation of words. In addition, the therapist can teach the hearing-impaired person a way to extend their voice quality and tone. They can also instruct them on how they can actively "listen" using body gestures and position.

In the past students with hearing impairments were educated in self-contained programs and in state supported residential schools. Today, most hearing-impaired students are taught in inclusive settings. One of the most positive changes in this field of education is the elimination of the term "deaf and dumb," which was used exclusively in the initial recognition of this condition. The term hearing impaired has more positive acceptance today.

Another positive change in the education of the hearing impaired is the focus on early intervention. Early stimulation programs are prevalent throughout the United States today, and the results indicate that they are essential in minimizing the difficulties imposed by hearing loss. The hearing-impaired child should participate in intensive intervention as an infant and continue with services throughout all other grades in school as needed. Parents should play an active role in the training so they can implement techniques at home. The earlier the diagnosis is made and appropriate training has started the better are the child's chances for developing language and speech skills.

There are three separate educational formats currently used with hearing impaired children today.

1. <u>American Sign Language (ASL)</u> is a unique visual language used by the American deaf culture. It uses hand sign and

symbols as the main method of communication. It is considered the primary language, and it places English as the second language.

2. The aural-oral approach stresses the development of a "natural" auditory-based language through training in the use of residual hearing with amplification. It is supplemented, if necessary, with speech reading.

3. The total communication approach combines auditory and oral training with a visual signed English system.

Hearing-impaired children are served by the IDEA, and thereby receive support and services from federal tax dollars for their education. They are eligible for an I.E.P. and may request the use of an interpreter in the class. (An interpreter is a person who is trained to enhance communication for the hearing impaired.). Hearing-impaired children are served in a variety of placements from self-contained classroom programs in their public school, to mainstreamed programs in public schools to residential schools. A large majority of the hearing-impaired children will need continual support in normal language development and acquisition. At the postsecondary level there are a variety of options including Gallaudet University in Washington, D.C., which is a four year liberal arts college that enrolls only hearing-impaired students. There are many community colleges and universities across the United States offering special services for the hearing impaired.

With the support of technology, hearing-impaired students can be served in almost any environment today. Technological advances have provided exciting alternatives for the hearing impaired. The hearing-impaired person will benefit from TDDs (telecommunication devices for the deaf). These portable units are easy to carry, inexpensive and are now available in most schools, businesses, shopping areas, hospitals, police and fire stations. These allow hearing impaired people direct access to services. Closed captioned television programming has allowed many hearing-impaired individuals to enjoy television and movies. The computer has been a wonderful communication link for the hearing impaired population, particularly the area of electronic mail. Along with the main benefits from receiving information without the use of oral language are the social benefits from being able to communicate on a far more regular basis with non-hearing and hearing friends. There are several electronic "CHAT" rooms set up where hearing-impaired individuals can reach out and "talk" with others.

The necessity for visual skills in the field of computer science makes the computer the critical tool for most hearing-impaired individuals today. The hearing-impaired person will continue to benefit from new technology as the "written word" becomes the communication tool of the decade. The implementation of new cochlear surgical implants and the use of laser techniques may help the hearing impaired in the future.

Learning Disabilities

The term learning *disabilities* was first coined by Dr. Sam Kirk. The term refers to a heterogeneous group of difficulties in acquiring and using skills for listening, speaking, reading, writing, reasoning, or math calculation and application. Learning disabilities include such conditions as dyslexia (reading), dysgraphia (spelling/writing) and dyscalculia (arithmetic).

The official description of this disorder has been documented since 1968, but we know that learning disabilities have existed for centuries. Programs supporting students with learning disabilities have been in our public schools since the 1960s. The incidence of this population is thought to be approximately 4 to 6 percent of the total school population. Approximately half of all children receiving special education services are classified as learning disabled.

Learning disabilities may occur with other conditions (e.g., ADHD or emotional disturbance) or with environmental factors (cultural differences or insufficient instruction). However, they are not the result of these influences. The individual's difficulty in learning is not primarily due to visual or hearing deficits, mental retardation, emotional disturbance, or economic, environmental or cultural disadvantage.

Most children with learning disabilities are diagnosed around second grade, but there is a push from parents and educators to begin to identify the disability sooner. The disorder is diagnosed as a result of the child's performance on a psycho-educational test battery. This test battery includes intellectual cognitive tests (IQ) and achievement tests in academic areas. The specialist tests to see if a severe discrepancy exists between the individual's apparent potential for learning and their present level of achievement.

Learning disabilities are life long. You do not outgrow your disability, but rather, learn a way to cope with it. The goal of the treatment plan is to help the individual learn new strategies to manage their dysfunction. Individuals with learning disabilities certainly can *learn*— they just learn *differently!*

Certain criteria must be met for a child to qualify for support and interventions for a learning disability within the public school. To determine if these criteria are met, the child is referred to a child study team at the school. This team of school professionals suggests interventions to help the child in the classroom. If success is not forthcoming, then the school psychologist is asked to do an observation and psycho-educational testing. If the results of this testing indicate that the student has a learning disability, he or she will be eligible for services from the school district. These services include individual help within the regular classroom, a self-contained classroom or a resource room where a specialist works directly with the child and in small groups for short periods of time during the day. This specialist will introduce a variety of educational strategies to enable the student to cope with the disability.

In addition to this initial testing, the student is eligible every three years for updated testing. Depending on the results of successive evaluations, the child may have the right to special instruction throughout elementary school, middle school and high school. In the area of higher education or postsecondary programs, there are college programs for learning disabled students available throughout the United States. Further, the post secondary student with a learning disability is eligible for support in the work place. The rights of students with learning disabilities are guaranteed by the Americans with Disabilities Act (ADA), which protects all disabled persons.

Treatment for students with learning disabilities includes intensive remediation in the specific academic area in which weaknesses exist. The school devises an I.E.P. for each student and the learning disability teacher, who is certified in strategy-based instruction along with the student's regular education teachers, are responsible for implementing the plan. Accountability is required and as skills are mastered, they are documented. At times, parents may choose to provide even more help outside of school with additional special instruction, but this is usually at their own expense. Some families seek private schools that work exclusively with children with learning disabilities. The Landmark School and College in Vermont and the Lab School in Washington, D.C. are two such specialized schools. Many others exist in communities across the country.

Future research in the area of learning disabilities is focusing on hereditary patterns within families. Parents will often tell evaluators " I had these difficulties when I was in school." Recently, G. Reid Lyon, a leading researcher in the field of learning disabilities, has suggested the presence of chromosome six as significant in children who had severe reading and decoding difficulties. The future for this field of chromosome studies will depend on new data from the major new treatment initiatives being sponsored by the National Institute of Child Health and Human Development. As the data from these studies is obtained, additional treatment plans will be possible.

Speech and Language Problems

Do you remember your child's first words? The chances are you do and you even recorded those words in a baby book. Your own children will be no different with your grandchild's first words. No doubt you will receive a call or a taped message sharing the very first utterance! At eight months most children make babbling sounds and then only a few months later you hear the first attempt at words. Then the vocabulary seems to explode and by 18 months the child is beginning to put words together into the first two-word sentences! Language development may appear so simple and obvious at first, but it is a very sophisticated and complex process.

Speech refers to how sounds are produced and formed into words. Language refers to the meaning, use and structure of what is expressed (spoken or written). Children can have a speech and/ or language problem.

All of us recognize when speech is unintelligible or when people have difficulties communicating their thoughts. That is because speech and language assume a pivotal role in everyday settings. Language is the major vehicle for transmitting ideas, feelings and information to others. Therefore, it is a critical life skill. We recognize its importance in social interaction and the influence it has on learning many new skills including reading, memory and motor development. Language provides the means through which one can problem solve. Those who find success in the academic and social world are more likely to assimilate and adapt their language skills.

There are marked individual differences in the rate at which children develop language with some indication that girls develop slightly more rapidly in the early years. Children who cannot speak and who use language differently from their peers will struggle to fit in. Children with limited language are at risk for academic subjects such as reading and begin to have social challenges when their peers begin to notice their efforts to talk. In short, school will be a frustrating experience for students with speech and language delays or deficits.

A problem in speech, language or hearing may be the child's only problem, or it may co-occur as a primary or secondary problem with another condition such as mental retardation, learning disability, or attention deficit hyperactivity disorder. Speech challenges involve the faulty production of sounds and the sound system itself.

These disorders are of four kinds:
1. phonological
2. articulation
3. fluency
4. voice

All four involve muscle movements of the speech production mechanism—the tongue, jaw, lips, etc. Some speech problems are severe, others are more mild. In all cases, the life of a speech de-layed child can be enriched once full communicative competence is achicved.

Fluency disorders (cluttering or stuttering) are another type of speech difficulty. In ancient times there are known reports of children who stuttered or had difficulty communicating despite normal hearing and intelligence.

Researchers are still debating the cause of stuttering. Some theories include environmental, neurological, and psychological factors that may cause stuttering. The dysfluency (or stuttering) often increases in high-pressured situations (e.g., speaking in front of an audience, talking on the phone). It is important that you don't tell the child to "slow down" or make him/her feel self-conscious about dysfluent moments. Modeling a slow and easy rate of speech is effective. Wait patiently when your grandchild experiences a dysfluent moment to provide a non-threatening environment.

In modern times, the first documented support for children with speech and language difficulties came in 1888 by a Viennese scholar Rafael Coen. Coen encouraged the very first movements of remediation of children with language challenges. Public school programs began to appear in the 1920s but were not widespread until the 1960s. In the first efforts to help children with language problems, support was offered only in the area of articulation ,voice quality and fluency. Trained specialists worked individually on these skills. In the past 20 years, however this school of thought has evolved and now the studies in children's language development have encouraged therapy in the areas of processing of language, the formation of language in a communicative practical way (prag-matics) and the ability to put words together and form sentences (syntax).

Parents who suspect their child has a speech or language difficulty may request a language screening for their child through the local public school or they may choose to have the testing done privately at their own expense. The professional most involved with the language delayed child will be the speech-language pathologist. This professional is highly trained and specializes in working with speech and language remediation.

After an evaluation, the speech-language pathologist will determine the type of program the child needs and explain it thoroughly to the parents. An individual speech plan will be written, and parents are encouraged to add their input. The instruction will differ in time and content depending upon the child's specific needs. Typically, the child will leave the classroom for a specified amount of time (e.g., twice a week for 30-minute sessions) and work with the clinician. The help may be offered one to one or in small groups. However, in a growing number of schools today, the speech-language pathologist may be working with the teacher in the classroom and helping the child within the classroom setting. The clinician will set up an individual treatment plan and annually test and evaluate to determine the child's progress. Parents will be notified of results and progress on a regular basis. A successful speech and/ or language program depends on close communication between the classroom teacher, the parents and the clinician.

Since 1975, speech-language pathologists have been included in the educational management of children with language disabilities. Prior to that year, speech-language pathologists provided help for the student but were independent of the educators. Children left the classroom and worked with the speech-language pathologist but there was little communication with the classroom teacher. Now speech- language pathologists participate in I.E.P. conferences with parents and members of the educational team. Therapy goals and activities are specified and shared. Successful communication skills are part of the child's overall educational management plan.

Two major changes are underway for the area of language communication. The first change is in the area of technology.

The second change is cultural. In the area of technology, improvements in technical devices to support speech and language disorders have advanced quickly. Augmentive communication devices for those with limited or no speech have helped the more severely delayed to use pictures or written words as a way to communicate. Computer software for instruction of language and remediation is another recent area providing support. Recent programs such as *FAST FORWARD*™ use the computer to help the child begin to process and use language in a more productive way. *Write and Talk*™, a software program, provides an oral communication program for the child who can talk but can't write well. Synthesized speech presentations to accompany visual presentations are now being offered along with software programs that train actual speech production and oral motor skills.

The second change is in the area of cultural experiences. This is particularly evident in the field of bilingual education. Bilingual education is for children who do not speak English as a native language. Spanish speakers are the largest and fastest growing minority language group in the United States. Speech and language therapy traditionally avoids teaching English as a second language but avoidance is becoming increasingly difficult as responsibilities increase. Speech-language pathologists have special expertise in communication so it is inevitable that they will be asked to assist children who are not competent in English. Today many pathologists are becoming certified in teaching bilingual classes and offering their expertise to children who are trying to master two languages. We are seeing a slow trend in the United States to begin to develop programs for children to learn more than one language. These issues continue to impact our educational system and each school system presently offers their own interpretation of how best to serve this population.

Thanks to the dedication of well- trained speech-language pathologists and the creative use of materials to enhance communication, the majority of speech and language impaired youngsters can develop skills and progress through the therapy program with success. The end result is that they will develop the ability to express their ideas and needs in a socially and developmentally appropriate manner. All children who need services are eligible, regardless of parental income or ethnic status, and today's wide range of techniques allows clinicians to design intervention programs that meet the child's needs.

Tourette's Syndrome / Tic Disorders

Tourette's syndrome is named for one of the first professionals who recorded the symptoms, Gilles de la Tourette, in 1885. This syndrome is described as an involuntary tic disorder (both motor and vocal tics) that occurs before the age of 18. A tic is described by the DSM-IV as a sudden, rapid, recurrent nonrhythmic, stereotyped motor movement or vocalization. The onset is typically between two and fourteen years of age.

Tourette noted the strong hereditary course of the syndrome and felt that the exact course of the disorder was very hard to predict. Modern research indicates that there is a strong familial history of tics including the probability of both maternal and paternal history of the disorder. Learning disabilities and attention disorders are relatively common among children with Tourette's.

Generally the motor tics are seen before the vocal tics. Tic disorders occur more commonly in males than females with a reported sex ratio of nine to one. The population is recorded as 59 per 10,000 births (Comings, 1990).

Children affected with tic disorders have variable tics such as grunts and vocalizations. Examples of tics include eye blinking, arm jerks, protrusion of the tongue and facial grimacing. Some children and adults talk about feeling an "urge" or "intensified rushed" sensation before the tic occurs. Whenever the tics occur, they disrupt the normal pattern of life, giving children with tics a sense of not being in control of their actions. Tics increase and diminish in severity over weeks to months. Some relief from the tic syndrome is possible with medication.

In Tourette's syndrome, one of the more unusual tics noted is the onset of compulsive swearing. It is one of the syndrome's most "theatrical" symptoms. Family members, friends and teachers have a great deal of difficulty with this particular symptom and may punish the child unfairly. The frequency of the tic is then impacted by the stress caused by punitive management at home or in the classroom and by the ridicule of peers. Tic disorders often affect self-worth, peer acceptance, school and/or job performance and family life.

The child with Tourette's is eligible for support and services under Section 504 of the Rehabilitation Act of 1973. This support should include reasonable accommodations that will offer the child some protection and understanding of this syndrome. Typically, a resource specialist or school psychologist will inform teachers and faculty working with the child of the implications of the disorder. Confidentiality is always a consideration as it is for all children with disabilities. However, general information can prevent some of the social reactions that may result without understanding the disorder. Some educators, who do not understand the disorder, punish the child for outbursts and actions. They think these behaviors are purposely produced by the child to disrupt and interrupt the classroom. Education of faculty and others involved with the student can reduce this type of unfortunate misunderstanding. If the child is also eligible for other services due to another disorder, such as learning disabilities, then the child will receive the typical resources available to all students.

An important issue for family members to understand is how stress or anxiety can make the tics more pronounced. Therefore, it is critical for family members to help protect the child from situations that would aggravate the tics. This is one way where grandparents can play a role in helping the child receive some relief from high anxiety situations in the family life.

If the syndrome is interrupting the daily life pattern of the child or the adult, medication is often suggested as a part of the treatment program. The drug selected is managed by the physician or psychiatrist and generally falls in the area of medications called dopamine receptors. Typical medications used to treat this syndrome include Haldol™ and Catapres™. Dr. David Comings, a leading researcher in this disorder, believes medication is effective in approximately 60 percent of the cases he sees. He notes that most patients are delighted with the decrease in their tics; they usually report the remaining tics are easier to live with. Patients often have to be reminded to stay on their medication indefinitely as the symptoms often reoccur once the medication is stopped.

Following medication, the next intervention typically introduced is family therapy. This is a type of intervention where the entire family meets with a therapist. Together as a team, they develop ways to handle discipline within the family unit and understand how this disorder affects the family dynamics. Behavior modification techniques and a behavior program using rewards, contracts and consequences seem to be helpful. The family needs to understand that although the child cannot be made responsible for the tics, they are responsible for all other inappropriate antisocial behaviors. Therefore it takes a skilled therapist to help a family begin to see how these strategies can work in their lives.

Future studies in genetics, neurochemistry, brain structure and function will continue to contribute to the understanding of the causes of this disorder. New research in DNA may help map the gene pattern of Tourette's syndrome for future generations. One recent study at the National Institute of Medical Health has focused on the autoimmune onset of streptococcal infections. This study is called PANDAS (pediatric autoimmune neurological studies). It is felt that this streptococcal infection may break down a chemical in the brain, which causes a repeated pattern in the brain to occur. It appears in the future that correcting this chemical imbalance combined with supportive therapy will be some of the key factors in a treatment plan for the individual with Tourette's syndrome.

Vision Impairments

A visually-impaired child has a measured loss of any of the visual functions such as acuity, visual fields, color vision or binocular vision. Children who are born with the disorder are said to be *congenitally* visually impaired. Congenital describes a condition present at birth but not limited to hereditary factors. Other children who acquire a visual loss later in life are *adventitiously* blind. Adventitious conditions are typically acquired after birth as the result of an accident or injury. The term *legally* blind refers to anyone with a visual acuity of 20/200 or worse in the better eye, with best correction or a peripheral field loss that is restricted to 20 degrees or less. The prevalence figure for the legally blind school-age populations is estimated at one legally blind student in 2,000 school children. It is estimated that 80 percent of this population have sufficient residual vision to use it as a primary learning channel. Today approximately 80 percent of the students with visual limitations participate in mainstreamed classes (regular education classrooms). The remaining 20 percent are in residential schools for the visually impaired or in home schooling situations.

Children with vision difficulties were given support long before the laws for disabled children and adults were enacted. Original educational opportunities consisted of state residential schools. Some school districts provide self–contained classrooms. Today the average visually-impaired student is in a regular education classroom with support from a vision specialist. Many public and private agencies and organizations offer support services or provide specialized materials and equipment for visually-impaired individuals. The use of books on tape have been offered exclusively for the vision-impaired population as have talking books, large type books and books in Braille. Also available to this population have been adaptive devices such as the cane and navigational electronic devices. Approximately 4 percent of the legally blind population desire and qualify for training to use specially trained dogs to provide support and independence to the individual.

The student with vision impairments is eligible for services within the public school. Special education services must span the full spectrum from infancy and preschool intervention to elementary and high schools. In addition, the education will include prevocational, vocational and transitional programs. The overall curriculum and standards will not be different for the child with visual impairments but will offer adaptive instruction and accommodations. These adaptations and accommodations may include access to printed or typed materials through an optical character recognition device, synthetic speech devices, computer monitors and printers in Braille, large print or synthesized speech.

Many visually-impaired young adults have a poorly developed self-concept. This is not a result of the actual vision impairment but rather results from the young adults lack of interaction with others in their environment. The visually-impaired young adult is often ignored by others and treated as unapproachable and helpless. These negative reflections hamper the social acceptance and self-esteem of the visually-impaired person. Concentrated efforts must be made in the lives of these students to increase their interactions with their peers and to educate others about their strengths and abilities.

Preventive programs to detect early vision problems and referral for special treatments are now available. The National Society to Prevent Blindness has developed an active prevention program. The society has identified that in one year alone 175,000 school children suffered eye injuries (90 percent of which could have been prevented if safety materials and special eye care guidelines were followed). Technology has certainly enhanced the quality of life and expanded the opportunities available to visually-impaired persons. New products, including paperless Braille machines and adapted microcomputers and electronic navigational instruments, have permitted the visually-impaired student to be more independent. New techniques and research in laser eye surgery and cornea transplants have opened up a new area of vision restoration.

Chapter Five
Accepting the Term Disability:
It Comes with the Package!

"Coming together is a beginning; keeping together is progress; working together is success."—Henry Ford

For some people, the hardest part of accepting a person with a disability is accepting the actual label defining the difficulty. Some consider the very name of the disability a negative. One grandmother said to her family " He isn't learning disabled, he is just a little boy! Don't let them label your son that way!"

We must understand that for the child to receive special support and help, which is often critical to success under our current law, the child's disability must be identified and labeled. The specific label describes the disability and allows the programs and services to be put into effect to begin to help the child. For example, if the school and parents recognize that the child has a learning disability, then that child receives free resource support from a trained specialist, testing and periodic re-evaluation. The help may include transportation to and from school and other related services such as occupational therapy and speech therapy. Those services are funded by federal tax dollars which are marked specifically for special needs students. Without the specific identification of "learning disability," the services would not be offered.

Acceptance of the label does not mean that you are giving up on the child. The label does not define the child. It only describes a part of the child's behavior or ability. Labels only serve our need to communicate. They do not reflect a final judgment. Definitions and labels only help us serve the needs of special children. They are subject to change and variance. Rather than focusing on the label, educate yourself as to what schools can and will provide for disabled students.

Thanks to concerned families and thousands of dedicated teachers speaking up over 25 years ago, our federal government passed laws protecting the rights of disabled students. One of these laws, the Individual Disability Education Act (IDEA), mandates that no child with a disability will be refused the right to a free and appropriate public education in our schools. Remember, your tax dollars, in part, support this law.

How a "Label" Can Serve Your Grandchild

Let's look at how your grandchild might get help under a *"label."* We will examine a situation that could be typical in any school district in the United States today. Let us imagine that your own children are concerned about your grandchild's ability to read. They have provided outside tutoring help, and everyone in the family, including you, has been working with the child. However, the child is still not reading successfully. Your children ask the school to review their child's progress. The teacher agrees that a challenge exists and moves first to discuss it with a panel of teachers (often called a child study team). This team suggests possible classroom interventions that may be of help, and the teacher then tries to implement these techniques with your grandchild. Following a reasonable amount of time, if a problem still exists then the teacher will request that a school psychologist observe the child. Once the psychologist has observed the child in the classroom, your children may be notified that the school would like to test the child to get a better idea of the child's skills and abilities. Parents are asked to sign a specific form at this time granting permission for testing. Once testing has been completed, a multi-disciplinary team meeting is held and your children will be requested to attend. At this meeting they will hear the results of this evaluation. If the tests indicate that the child's reading problem is due to a learning disability, then a variety of suggestions and interventions are made. It is now up to your children to accept or reject, in writing, these suggestions. Should they agree, a legal document, called the Indi-

66

vidual Education Plan (I.E.P.), is designed to identify what strategies will be implemented. An I.E.P. is a multi-form document that states the child's disability, shares the testing documentation to prove the disability and then lists goals and objectives for the school to employ to help the child succeed. The I.E.P. requires the signature of everyone present at the meeting, including the parents or guardians. Without the parents' direct permission no help or support in the classroom will be given. Once signed, this document will be placed into the child's permanent record and will be a part of his or her school plan. The plan is subject to annual review and all parties are present at this review. School personnel will check to see if your grandchild has mastered the objectives of the plan. This process is used in every public school in the United States. Once the I.E.P. is in place, your grandchild may be on the pathway to learning new strategies to help him or her cope with the disability.

This is the way the process should work. From the initial placement of services on, the team will update the parents regularly and let them know the child's progress. See the table that follows for a visual map of this process. This program was set into motion by everyone recognizing that the child would benefit from additional support. You can foster the parents in their understanding of this and salute them for their "active" parenting.

If you are the legal guardian of your grandchild, you will be the person to whom all inquiries and information are directed regarding the child's needs in school. If you have custody of your grandchild and you believe he or she needs help or testing you must put this request in writing. In a brief letter, state your guardianship and then the reasons why you are requesting testing or support for your grandchild. This request is first directed to the child's classroom teacher. *Keep a copy of all requests you send to the school.* The teacher shares this letter with school personnel, including the school psychologist, and you should receive a response as to the results of your request within 45 calendar days. The process described above is highlighted in the following table.

Steps for Identifying Children with Special Needs in Schools

1. Request of testing by parents or guardian
2. School must respond in 45 days
3. Teachers meet and devise a action plan of interventions
4. If no changes occur after interventions are tried school psychologist starts formal assessment with parents approval
5. Results of testing are shared to entire team, including parents or guardian
6. If child is found eligible for special education and related services under I.D.E.A. an individual educational plan (I.E.P) is designed to meet child's needs. Related services are offered if needed
7. If child is not eligible for special education and related services, but is found to have a disability, the child may receive accommodations in the regular education program under Section 504 of the Rehabilitation Act of 1975
8. If child is not eligible for special education and related services or Section 504 accommodations, interventions in the regular classroom environment should be implemented to assist the child
9. If the parents or guardians disagree with the school's findings they may follow due process procedures

Understanding Related Services—Who Are All These People Anyway?

Once a child has been identified as having special needs and as being eligible for special education and related services the school team will begin to designate specific services. These services are documented in the I.E.P. and will be offered on a timely basis to the child. The services are part of the free and appropriate educational program for all children.

Sometimes parents feel overwhelmed when they are working with so many professionals on the child's team. They may begin to undermine their own confidence in whether they can care for the child themselves. Caring professionals should recognize that they must be cooperative and understanding when they work with parents of disabled youth. As a grandparent, you may want to be present at these initial meetings just to show your support and involvement in the family and to act as another set of "eyes and ears" for communication later. Several of the grandparents that I have worked with carry tape recorders to these meetings to help the family review what was discussed in the meeting. Families working with professionals in a collaborative effort can develop more comprehensive and appropriate care plans that are mutually beneficial to all. The most effective plans are individually tailored to the child's strengths and needs.

Some of the specific services available to children with special needs in the public school may include the following:

- speech and language therapy
- occupational therapy
- physical therapy
- the services of a diagnostic specialist
- testing by a school psychologist
- adaptive physical education
- support from a paraprofessional or teacher aid
- behavioral intervention services
- services from an orientation mobility specialist
- health services
- learning disability resources
- tutoring services
- vision assistance/services

School-based professionals who will work with your grandchild individually or include him or her in small groups with other typical students provide these services. Each professional will have goals for helping the child and will speak with the family regarding interventions and objectives. Below are brief descriptions of the professionals with whom you will work.

Speech-language pathologist. The trained pathologist will work individually or in small groups with your grandchild. Typical areas of focus include articulation of speech, stuttering, expressive and receptive language, pragmatic language and central auditory processing difficulties. The pathologist will set up goals for the student to master and will inform the parents on a regular basis of the child's progress.

Occupational therapist. This specialist will offer support to the individual alone or in a group format for developing fine and gross motor skills. They will often suggest a home program parents can use to continue the techniques.

Physical therapist. This therapist works on the more involved motor activities such as using a wheelchair and developing strategies for muscle control.

The diagnostic specialist. This person will evaluate the child and offer specific strategies and interventions for the classroom teacher to implement. They may also test the child and determine strengths and weaknesses.

School psychologist. This professional will evaluate cognitive (learning) and achievement (acquired skills) for each child. They will determine what programs the child may be eligible for based on their testing. They often serve as the manager or head of the multi-disciplinary team meeting in the school.

Adaptive physical educator. This is trained physical education teacher. A program will be developed to adapt physical activity to the child's needs and help the child develop alternative methods of exercise and motor development.

Paraprofessional. This person is a support to the child under the direction of the classroom teacher. Paraprofessionals are trained by the school district. They are non-certified staff who will work one-on-one with children who need additional support and assistance during the school day.

Behavior intervention specialist. Specialists in this category are persons who are trained in behavior techniques. They work directly with the teacher and school psychologist to implement behavior programs and help the child develop self–control.

Orientation mobility specialist. This professional helps the student adapt to life outside of school prior to graduation. Practical life skills for developing an independent life style are taught. This specialist will work with the student to practice taking public transportation, opening a bank account, keeping household records, and a variety of life skills.

School nurse. These medically trained professionals are school-based practitioners who are responsible for administering medications, shots as required, and vision and hearing screenings. They are part of the multi-disciplinary team.

Learning disability specialist. This is a master level trained educator who employs techniques and strategies to help the student with learning challenges. He or she is employed in every school district in the country. This resource teacher will offer small group instruction with typical students either in a separate room or within the classroom.

Tutor. This is a certified teacher who is often hired by the family to support the child outside of school. The tutor will help with homework and daily lessons from school. Tutors frequently see the child one or two times a week after school.

Vision specialist. This is a specially trained special education teacher who works with students who have vision deficits. The role of the specialist is to provide either direct or indirect instruction for the visually-impaired student. This person will procure materials needed, work with teachers and other personnel involved with the child in the school. This specialist will also develop compensatory or adaptive skills required by the visually-impaired child to function effectively in school and society.

This review of services and support within the school and community should be helpful to you in understanding the "maze" of services and programs available to children who qualify for such assistance. Although this information can seem overwhelming, remember you will only be looking at one small piece of it with your own grandchild. This list represents the entire scope of services and most children will use only a few of these resources.

The field of education is constantly changing. The value of laws, regulations and services for students with disabilities are continually challenged. Some people feel that these laws have exposed the inadequacies and contradictions of public education. Therefore, it is critical to stay current about local laws and interpretations of these laws for the special needs student. New information from research should and will continue to change the education your grandchild is receiving. Parents and grandparents will need to be able to recognize and insist that the most current support is available for their children. Close and frequent communication with the child's school is a must for parents in fostering success within the public school system for their child. Most schools, clinics, agencies and support groups genuinely welcome attendance at meetings or school activities by grandparents.

We know that the fields of health, medicine, social work, psychology, education and others have made great strides in the treatment, documentation, and support of children with disabling conditions. However, these advances may at times be overwhelming to a family and not specific to their day-to-day needs and challenges. We must remember that regardless of their handicapping conditions, your grandchildren have the same needs as typical children. Challenges do not stop their natural desire to grow, to develop into strong adults, to be accepted, to belong, to be loved and to love.

What to Look for in a Typical Educational Program

When your children or you as the caregiver seek the best possible educational environment for your special needs child , first look to your local public school. As taxpayers we have the right to receive a free and appropriate public education for our youth. Some school districts do an outstanding job of working with special needs youngsters. Others have a different agenda and the services are less than satisfactory. Be aware of where the outstanding special education districts are in your state. Your local state department of education may be able to guide you and your family in selecting where you can move in the community to benefit from such services. On the other hand, your family can seek the personal advice of a local support group member who is experienced with the local schools and what they offer. Do not assume that all public schools are equal in service. Seek out the area where the special needs child will receive the best education and the best that your tax dollar can provide. There are many outstanding special private schools that should also be explored. These charge tuition but may be an option for some families. One drawback to private specialized schools for disabilities is that the children at the school all have a disability. This makes it a restricted learning environment without exposure to typical students and students of diversity. Each family will have to make a choice of what works best for the welfare of their child.

If you feel that the school district has failed to provide adequate services for you grandchild, you have the right to ask for a mediator (free of charge) to review the case and render an opinion. This service is provided under the special education law. Information regarding this service can be obtained by a request to the director of special education within the school district office.

Chapter Six
How You Can Help

"Crises refine life. In them you discover what you are."—Allan K Chalmers

Your own children, the parents of the special needs child in your family, will experience their own personal difficulties in coping with their child's condition. Regardless of the cause, parents tend to blame themselves and may experience periods of guilt and depression. For some, when they hear the initial diagnosis, it is as if their personal dreams for the child have been taken away. You can offer your positive spirit and encouragement to help them see the many possibilities and avenues of hope available for them and their child. This chapter will deal with many ways for you to become the guiding light in your family and in the life of your grandchild.

Personal

First and foremost the best present you can give your grandchild is the gift of your time. Time for listening to a long story, time to wait patiently as he or she tries to ride their two-wheeler, time to sit beside the child and wait when his or her parents are delayed. Being with your grandchild in an open, relaxed way will create memories of wonderful times together. You have the time to really enjoy your grandkids, to be there and to really listen. Today's parents have so much to do. Grandkids will remember that you are not too busy to listen.

Tips for Good Listening

1. When you are listening to a child, concentrate on the child's feelings and message.
2. Make positive eye contact, follow the child closely with

your eyes, without interrupting the conversation.
3. Be alert to feelings that the child is expressing.
4. Lean forward to show your interest.
5. Nod frequently and show both verbally and with nonverbal gestures that you empathize with the feelings expressed behind the words.
6. When you respond, stay on the child's topic.
7. Attend to what the child said. Initially, avoid adding comments about your own experiences that were similar.
8. Show that you are there to listen and let the child expand and explore his ideas as you learn from the child.

These loving "quiet" gifts of time are the ones most appreciated. When you think back later on your conversation with the child, you will feel that you provided encouragement by your active listening. To your grandchild, just listening is more important than what you send or what you write and talk about. Remember, no matter how old your grandchild is, the *wise* grandparent realizes that being available to listen your grandchild is a priority.

Grandparent as a Childcare Provider

One activity most grandparents enjoy is caring for their grandchild when the parents need to work long hours, attend a special function, go on a business trip or just have a break from the routine. These times can be too few for some grandparents and too frequent for others. Having a child with special needs often adds to the daily rigors of life. The special needs child often requires special attention from outside professionals, more meetings with schools, visits to physicians, etc. Their parents may provide more support in the child's day than in a typical child's week or month. The opportunity for parents to have relief from the all–encompassing demands of a special child is extremely important. Therefore, your role as a babysitter (for young grandchildren) or as the provider of childcare (for older grandchildren) may take on different dimensions. Your ability to relieve your children is a real act of support. Decide early on how much time you will allow to this, if at all. Childcare is not a requirement of grandparenting. It is a service you can offer to help the family ease their stress and frustration. How you approach this with your children depends on your open communication with them about your own personal life and your choices. Each grandparent will need to find their own comfort zone in the area of how much time they can give to childcare. Considerations must be given to the time spent on the activity. Financial obligations must also be considered. If you are responsible for a large part of the child's care, what remuneration can be offered to you for pulling you out of the work force? If you choose not to care for your child, will you later feel guilty about this? Regardless of what arrangements your grandchild will need, you must know your intentions in the relationship right from the start. Avoid being angry with the family because they "expect me to provide childcare all the time" if you did not make your intentions known from the first place. Decide how much time you will give, if any, and let your children know up front so there are no preconceived feelings of guilt or discomfort. Ask yourself the following questions.

1. What are my personal needs for my time first and foremost?
2. What do I personally want to do in my life the next few years?
3. What are my own goals in my relationship with my grandchild?
4. What are my predicted personal financial needs over the next years?
5. How can I help with child- care in a fair way for all involved and still feel as though I am a supportive parent and grandparent?

When you can answer these questions honestly you will be ready to respond or to offer when your children ask you to provide childcare. Remember you are not responsible for the lives your adult children have chosen. *You can ease their burdens, but you cannot remove them.*

77

Behavior Issues

When you become active in your grandchild's life you will be his or her "teacher" in many ways. At times you will be with your grandchild when unacceptable behavior is observed. The special needs child is no different in their need for attention, be it negative or positive. Therefore, it behooves you to understand the discipline rules of your child's home and to maintain those rules when the child is with you even for a short time. You will keep the family avenue of communication open when you discipline the child in the same manner to which they are accustomed. The name of the approach is "proceed with a united front." Be sure you talk to your own children about what they expect when the child is with you. Discipline means "to teach" and teaching is something grandparents do all the time whether they realize it or not. Your goal as a grandparent is to teach a child to be considerate of other's feelings, to respect adult direction, and to be responsible for his or her feelings and behavior. Below are several strategies to guide you in behavior management.

1. Recognize positive behaviors first. Note when your grandchild is on task and doing what is expected of her and reward or praise immediately. Example: *"You know how to play with your little sister. I can see that when you take turns so nicely. It is fun to play games with you because you are a fair player."* In the words of one behavior specialist " Catch them being good!" Your praise does not have to be words; it can be a hug, a look or a wink. The important thing to do is to communicate what you respect about what they are doing. It is far more productive to reward children for positive behavior when they are exhibiting appropriate behavior. It is a different story when they are misbehaving.

2. Distract the child from the deviant behavior with another activity. This technique is called redirection. For example, you may redirect or reframe the child who is angry by quickly catching them off guard and encouraging them to look at something else. Example: *The child is bothering your dog and teasing the dog relentlessly. You ignore the behavior initially but the child goes*

on. You quickly call to the child and say, "John. Look at this new software game Grandpa has bought for the computer, can you help me put it in? It is so exciting, WOW! Look at this!" Suddenly what YOU are doing, your enthusiasm and interest, draw the child to the activity and away from the negative action.

3. Try ignoring misbehavior for awhile. When difficult behavior exists, and it will with any child at some time, immediately try to ignore the behavior first if the child is not physically harming themselves or another person. In short, pay attention to what they do that is correct, ignore what they do that it is NOT correct. The philosophy in ignoring is "if you don't pay attention to what I am doing I will stop it because my ultimate goal is that you will pay attention to me."

If ignoring does not produce a change in the behavior, then another step is in order. You might make a deal or write a contract with the child. Example: "If you stop bothering your sister, I will be able to take you to the library with me." The reward should be something the child desires, but it does not have to be a large monetary or material award. In fact, avoid things you cannot deliver. Offer reasonable rewards that are interesting to the child and which are short-term and easily attainable. Be alert and deliver the reward when the inappropriate behavior stops.

4. Use time-out to remove the misbehaving child from a situation. Dr. Russell Barkley, a psychologist who is known for writing books on managing oppositional behavior in children, recommends that for young children you use a chair placed outside of the room where you are when the misbehavior occurs. The child must sit on the chair for a brief period (he suggests one minute for each year of age) and the time is monitored by a stop-watch or kitchen timer. At the end of the time you join the child and explain why the child was "timed out" and what the child can do to avoid it again. This isolation period is a time in which the child can "cool down." For very active children the time must be adjusted, as even a minute in the chair may be too difficult. With very active children just a few seconds in the chair can seem like major punishment and may worsen misbehavior. Thus, for some of these chil-

dren a minute may prove almost impossible. If the behavior is extremely serious, you will want to involve parents for their input on how they would like you to proceed. If they are not readily available, you will want to remove the child to a room away from the altercation and sit with them during the brief time out. If the child runs out of the room, you will have to act quickly and bring them back. You may want to offer something for them to hold during time out like a "kush ball" (a small plastic string-like ball). Sometimes very active children just need something to hold while they are waiting and can often settle down faster when they are allowed this diversion. Eventually, offer a quiet game to play while the child attempts to "cool down." If your grandchild displays this type of upsetting behavior often, you will want to discuss thoroughly with his parents alternative consequences and other methods. There are some excellent reading materials about behavior challenges.

In his very popular book and video on child management, *1-2-3 Magic!*, Dr. Thomas Phelan teaches a simple behavior strategy that the entire family can use for children two to twelve. Dr. Russell Barkley, in his book, *Your Defiant Child*, and in his videos, *Understanding Defiant Behavior* and *Managing Defiant Behavior*, gives concrete strategies to help parents and teachers deal with very oppositional children. These books and videos are available in local bookstores or by contacting the A.D.D. WareHouse (800-233-9273).

Childproof Your Home

A recent *Dear Abby* column debated the pros and cons of grandparents child proofing their homes when their grandchildren visit. One side of the debate stated that the grandparent should have the right to keep all their special things out and displayed in their place. This side believes it is the child who needs to adjust and show respect. The other side debated that it was unfair to put the pressure on the child wherein they would feel uncomfortable and worried that they might destroy or hurt something in the grandparents' home.

As the grandparent of a special needs child you will want to think about your home and what kind of environment it provides for your visiting grandchild. The special needs grandchild may have physical limitations, which may make certain items in the home dangerous or very fragile for them to be near. For example, the blind or visually-limited child may find it initially difficult to find their way in your home and need to support themselves on the furniture. You would not want your home to be an obstacle course for this child. Their struggles with your environment might result in knocking things over and the child may get injured. Perhaps your special needs grandchild needs continual behavior support and encouragement. The temptation of special items in the room are like candy, making it hard for them to exhibit self-control. In these situations potential problems can be avoided by simply removing certain items in your home.

I believe you must take the child's unique needs into consideration and when they are visiting you should make every attempt to provide an atmosphere that is safe and protective for them as well as your belongings. One tragic incidence occurred in my state of Arizona where grandparents watching their grandchild did not provide protection around their family pool. The child slipped from their sight within the home and ran outside and entered the deep end of the pool. The child was unable to swim, and it was too late by the time the grandparents noticed she was missing. Adapting your surroundings is the most positive way to show your respect and concern for all involved. You are demonstrating for your children and grandchildren that you care enough to provide some changes in your home so they feel comfortable, accepted and safe.

In an effort to childproof your home, be sure you have a first aid kit with all appropriate equipment should a physical emergency arise. Include such items as oversized bandages, cough medicine for children and syrup of Ipec for accidental poisonings. Be sure you have emergency numbers by the phone. Ask parents for their family doctors' number and keep it in a handy place. In addition, if insurance cards can be duplicated for you to have available, this will be helpful if an emergency visit to the doctor or hospital is necessary.

Financial

Most grandparents who have financial resources and leisure time find great pleasure in the relationships they develop and the activities they share with their grandchildren. In many cases, grandparents have a more relaxed attitude toward their grandchildren than they had when they were young parents themselves. Tales of doting grandparents who indulge their grandchild's every whim are well known! Although these over indulgences are generated by the most loving of intentions, spoiling grandchildren can create some family disagreements. This is especially true for the special needs child who may have dietary restrictions or who is in need of special behavior management programs.

Grandparents can avoid disagreements by openly discussing expectations beforehand with the parents. Request careful explanations and guidelines for the child's care and write them down. These instructions may include using specific behavior strategies if the child acts out, diet limits, the use of medication, and encouraging the child to participate in activities which are most beneficial for the child. By being well-informed, grandparents will be able to provide consistent childcare and help whenever and where ever it is most needed.

A growing number of grandparents are becoming the sole financial supporters of their grandchildren. They are providing a home for their grandchildren, and it will be the "second time around" for them to parent. In many of these families the financial burden is a key issue. One in four grandparents raising their grandchildren live below the poverty level, which is less than $10,000 per couple, as reported by the Census Bureau in 1998. When a grandmother is the sole caretaker, that figure more than doubles.

If you have the financial responsibility for your grandchildren and if you are in financial need, you will be eligible for certain child-welfare benefits. Typically, this ranges from $150 to $225 per month. This is significantly lower, however, than what foster-care families receive ($500 to $600 per month). Because of this inequity, some states have implemented "kinship care" systems, which increase the stipend a relative can receive. To be eligible for these programs grandparents must relinquish their responsibility for the children over to the state. When this occurs the grandchild remains with the grandparent but social workers are assigned to the family. They are in charge of all decisions for the child including out of state travel, schooling and medical care. This may be uncomfortable for some grandparents who find it intrusive and perhaps creates the feeling of being watched. However, to receive the funding benefits, the grandparents must turn over this authority to the state.

Some grandparents are able to set up trusts or financial bequests for their grandchildren with special needs. Be careful that you understand your state's regulations on leaving sizable gifts to your grandchildren. The states have a mixture of legislation and case law that can be bewildering. Did you know there is even a federal law, that states "if you leave a person with special needs anything over $2,000 that person loses eligibility for all government benefits?" There are legal ways to protect against this $2,000 limit and specific financial ways to provide for a child's lifetime care, even if a family is not wealthy. Therefore, it is best to contact an attorney before you make such a gift known. In many states, having funds in one's own name disenfranchises the individual with a disability from vital services and benefits including Medicaid and Social Security Supplemental Income (SSI). Contact your attorney and ask for information regarding special needs estate planning.

Legal

Sometimes family situations arise where your children are unable to take care of your grandchildren. You may be advised or asked to take over the role as legal guardian. The condition of "guardianship" is pertinent to the rights of a child because it grants to one person, the guardian, the legal authority to make decisions for another, the ward. A lesser degree of decision-making is found in "limited guardianship" or "protectorship." It is a formalizing of the "benefactor" role for decision-making; it involves a partial rather than total delegation of personal control. Within limited guardianship a distinction is made between guardianship of the estate and guardianship of the person. The law allows the guardian to make a wide range of decisions for the ward (except financial). These guardianship laws again differ from state to state. If you are caring for your grandchild in your home, you may be eligible for a federal tax exemption. You must pay more of your dependent's expenses than they do, and certain income limitations apply to your dependent. Talk to your tax preparer.

Another way to stay involved with your special needs child's life is the role of *advocate*. This is not a legal relationship but more of a supportive relationship. You assume a role as an advocate on behalf of the child in his or her interactions with the agencies and schools that are working with him and providing services.

In some cases, after a divorce or disruption in a relationship, parents have withdrawn from grandparents the privilege of communicating with their grandchildren. Grandparents claiming their "rights" to stay connected with grandchildren in these disrupted families have started to appear in recent court rulings in a number of states.

Every state has laws setting out the rules for grandparents who wish to secure court-ordered time with their grandchildren. Recently several states have had cases where the courts have limited or invalidated these laws. In these states, the ruling declared that the grandparents visitation laws actually represented unwarranted government intrusion into parental matters. These laws have become more complicated than ever because of the growth of nontraditional households. It is common now for children to have more than two sets of grandparents competing for the interests of their grandchildren. This can be a potentially challenging circumstance for parents who find that they are involved with juggling several sets of grandparents. During the writing of this book (2000) a landmark case sits in the U.S. Supreme Court ready to determine such an issue. *Troxel vs. Granville* may potentially change grandparents' rights forever. Two grandparents from Seattle, Washington are in conflict with their daughter, who is the mother of their two grandchildren, for the right to spend time with the girls. The American Association of Retired Persons (AARP) is advocating the grandparents' rights and has filed a friend-of-the-court brief in support of the grandparent visitation. The court will hear arguments as to whether it is in the best interests of the child for visitation with their grandparents. The results of this case may impact relationships with families for years to come.

How can you manage if you are thrown into one of these difficult situations?

1. Focus on your grandchildren and not on the anger or feelings you have for their parents.

2. Try to avoid verbal conflict as much as possible. Be aware that the price of a battle with parents may result on emotional damage inflicted on the grandchildren.

3. Do everything you can within your power to work with the parents. Assure them that you do not want to undermine their authority and that your sole concern is your love for the child. Arthur Kornhaber, the author of *Grandparent Power!* suggests: "You have to work it out. You have to love a child more than you hate each other."

4. Suggest mediation. Mediation is when the situation is reviewed by an outside non–partial source who reviews all information from both sides and suggests an alternative. This is set up by an agency or court and provides a trained litigator to speak with all parties. The goal of mediation is to help everyone involved reach a conclusion that satisfies all parties.

5. Stay in close contact with all parties. Tape record meetings so you do not forget critical appointments and information. Keep informed and involved.

6. Update yourself with resources that are available and can offer you specific suggestions and guidance. Look at the Resource section of this book under the *National Coalition for Grandparents and The Foundation for Grandparenting* for their resources. These two groups can

give you current information and provide some valuable insight for your own personal issues.

Communication: Staying in Close Contact

In this day and age of mass communication a grandparent should always be able to communicate with their grandchild. From low discount family rates on the telephone, to postcards and preformed letters, digital cameras and video, to e-mail and interactive CDs, technology offers every opportunity to communicate. Even if you live across the globe, there are easy ways to be connected and available. Get involved with the computer e-mail system and you can chat on a regular basis with your grandchild. Try some of these suggestions.

1. Keep a colorful note pad right by the phone. Call it your "question pad" for when you speak with grandchildren. Jot down things you want to ask them when you are on the phone and write down things they mention or tell you they are planning so you can ask them later. They will be pleased that you remembered.

2. Purchase an easy-to-manage computer like an *IMAC* and get on e-mail. You can chat with your grandchild and other family members. Some creative families have set up entire web pages just for their family news.

3. Purchase postcards when you visit local museums. Jot down how you spent your day and mail it immediately. For a special occasion send your grandchild an album or photo box where he or she can keep the cards.

4. Once you have identified a special interest of your grandchild look for items in the newspaper or magazine that pertain to that interest. Clip a variety of these and send on to your grandchild periodically.

5. Use soft pack mailers and large postal delivery envelopes to send special games, fun notes and photos to your grandchild.

6. Copy stores today provide so many inexpensive projects you can make and send to your grandchild. Consider a calendar with pictures of last year's activities together as a

highlight of holiday giving. Collect a group of favorite pictures and laminate them into a placemat-sized sheet for the child to use at mealtime.

7. Make it a significant event to take a photo of your grandchild every year in the same place at around the same time (e.g., on their birthday, take a photo outside of the front door of their home). Get a special group photo frame and display the pictures. They will serve as a photo timeline of the child growing up.

8. Start a chain letter just for your grandchildren. Each child writes a few lines and sends the letter to the next grandchild on the list. When the last grandchild has added their comments it is sent back to you. Now include your comments and send it on to start again. A helpful hint is that when you start it around again you include stamps and even self-addressed envelopes so that it is easier for each child to continue the chain.

One outstanding resource for creating memories with your grandchildren is the book *Grandloving* by Sue Johnson and Julie Carlson. This activity book features more than 300 things you can do with your grandchild including many projects under $1. Check the resource section of this book for ordering information.

Family History: Making Memories for Grandchildren

With your knowledge of family history, now is the time when you should record information for future generations. It is important to establish bonds between the generations. You are in a unique position to pass along family history and provide this stability of roots. Take one day a week for an entire month and devote an hour or more on that day to the effort of recording your family history for the enjoyment of generations to come. Try these suggestions:

1. Draw a simple family tree and include information regarding all the members in your family from as far back as

your can remember. Include weddings and birthdays as you know them. Make copies of the family tree and give them to your children to add to their personal documents. Keep the original in your personal mementos.

2. If your own parents are still alive, use a video camera and interview them talking about their life and memories. If they are not, ask a friend to tape you sharing the information you remember about your family history and what you remember about your grandparents.

3. Collect old family photos and identify them with names and dates, if possible. Write the information on the back of the photos and store in acid-free envelopes.

4. Preserve on video important things from your life—not just photos. Gather a cluster of mementos that include personal belongings (e.g., uniforms, awards, mementos, medals, trophies, etc.) and video them all as a group. Record your voice as you film and describe the objects.

7. Consider the announcement of the pregnancy as a time to start a personal journal for the yet unborn grandchild. Create a daily diary until the day of birth where you record conversations with the parents of the child, thoughts and good wishes for the future, interesting tidbits about family history and the joy that surrounded the announcement of pending birth. Present the diary to the mother upon the birth of your grandchild. The journal will be given to the grandchild when they are old enough to appreciate it. If it is hard for you to start such a journal, there are some available in bookstores to help you such as *For My Child, A Mother's Keepsake Journal* or *A Father's Journal, Memories For My Child* both by author, Linda Kranz.

8. Tape record the voices of family members talking about important family events and amusing and interesting anecdotes regarding family members. It is often easy to do this when the family is gathered (e.g., at a wedding or christening). Label the tapes regarding their context and place them in a colorful box for gift giving. Present these tapes to your children on special occasions.

Gift Giving

For some grandchildren it is a true gift just having their grand-parents alive, well and able to be with them on a regular basis. For others it is knowing that their grandparents will take the time to select a special gift for them each year, or that they can rely on grandparents' monetary gifts on special occasions. For the special needs grandchild, gift giving could include things outside of the realm of normal gift choices. For example, you can pay the fees for a speech therapist to provide services beyond what the school can give, tuition for a special school, pay for a summer school class, arrange for transportation to a doctors appointment. Gifts do not have to be monetary in nature but should include free, creative and fun things.

One grandparent I know collects one dollar bills. Every time he receives change back he removes the one dollar bills and keeps them in a bank for when grandchildren visit. Whatever the sum is, they are allowed to remove it, divide it up equally and then spend it in a way they all can enjoy. Some of the ways they have used the money include renting a video, going to a fast food drive in and buying milk shakes for everyone and buying boxes of Girl Scout cookies, which they took to a senior retirement home. The value of grandparents is not measured by their material gifts alone but rather by the unconditional love they provide, the doors they open, the philosophy and heritage they hand down and their love for and belief in their grandchild's personal worth. Dr. Lillian Carson cautions grandparents to not "lose sight of the most meaningful and lasting gift of all, the one money can't buy—giving of your self." Here are two gift lists—one that involves low cost suggestions and the other more costly ideas to help generate some thoughts for your gift giving.

Creative and Inexpensive Gifts

1. A different packet of new pencils once a month for school—the pencils include grippers or pencil pillows often used

by kids who hate to write!

2. Colored highlighters, colored Post-its® and colored index cards to help the inattentive child focus and remember school work

3. Batteries for hearing aids, wheel chairs, special watches, other adaptive equipment.

4. Create books on tape. Tape record favorite stories for children. Send it to parents to use at night or quiet time for active youngsters.

5. Offer to be the regular driver to lessons, tutoring or doctor appointments.

6. Volunteer one day a week in your grandchild's school. Go to the school sport activities and start a grandparent support group at the school.

7. Provide the nametags for items, which are often lost.

8. Make a "coupon book." Make a list of 10 things you could do to help the family, from a day of childcare to making a meal, to doing yard work. Then make a coupon booklet and tell them they can redeem the coupons with you at any time.

9. Make some of the equipment that might be needed by the child including slant boards for writing, block for floor under desk where feet do not touch floor, soft pillows used for bed and chair comfort.

10. Visit on a Sunday and make all the lunches for the child for the week. This provides organization and help to families of disabled children who are often busy with so many daily activities.

11. Scheduling a weekly library visit where you pick up grandchildren and take them for an afternoon at the library. Select and read different books and magazines. Help them obtain library cards of their own.

12. Plan a super market shopping day. Allow your grandchild to carry their own list for several items and to select them and bring them back to the cart. Clip coupons and have them search for the item mentioned. Let them have the

experience of using a calculator to total their items. This is a great way to teach hands-on math skills.

13. Write to Pueblo, Colorado to the United States Information Center Resource address and obtain their catalog of free and inexpensive items. Select several items that you believe will be of interest to your grandchild. Send away for the items and request that they be sent directly to your grandchild. This may provide motivation and interest for the challenged student and *everyone* enjoys receiving mail!

14. Cut out bold headlines from the papers and ads in magazines. Paste in a notebook so child can practice reading different bold printed words. This is helpful for students with visual or reading difficulties.

15. If your grandchild is in elementary school, ask parents or teachers for a list of current sight words that the child is expected to know at that grade level. Copy words on colorful index cards and make a set of flash cards for the child. Store in an inexpensive recipe box. Provide for child to review when they are visiting.

More Costly Gifts

1. Costs for private evaluation and testing outside of what school provides.

2. Special camps and fees for school outings for special needs children.

3. Computers and computer equipment with software that is adapted to specific learning needs.

4. Financial remuneration to cover the costs for after school tutoring or special therapy beyond what the school offers.

5. Membership to special needs support groups and subscriptions to journals regarding research and interventions for special needs populations.

6. Consultation with an expert in the specific field of need.

7. Fees for parents to attend a special conference on the disability.

8. Provide a skilled caregiver from a respite service to come

in for a weekend and give parents a break.

9. Tuition to a private school for special needs.
10. Counseling or therapy with a behavior therapist or psychologist for entire family. This may include therapy for just the individual child.
11. Special adaptive equipment such as a no spill cup, protective helmet for head, tape recorder, Braille or talking watch, hand held personal speller, oversized keyboard for computer, talking calculator, etc.
12. Parents will enjoy books and magazine subscriptions that are specifically geared to the particular disability. For the child, magazine subscriptions to different children's magazines are especially helpful for disabled and unmotivated readers.

The fun part is coming up with the ideas for the gift. A wise grandparent openly discusses the choice of gifts with the parents, assuring that the gift is needed and wanted before presenting it. Many people regard gift giving as a hobby, and they actively try to seek gifts that they believe represent their own personal message. Above all, a gift should connect the giver in a personal way with the recipient. Do not lose sight of the fact that the best gift you can give is the gift of yourself. You have one thing you can give your grandchild that no one else can give them and that is your unconditional love.

Use Books to Teach About Special Needs

One personal way you can support your special needs grandchildren is by selecting books for them to read that contain a therapeutic message of support. Using books that provide this worthy message is called bibliotherapy.

Certain books carry an encouraging message of healing. Therapists often use books about real life concerns to help children understand a personal difficulty. Books that incorporate such messages attempt to model or illustrate how to cope with and handle a challenge. Find a specific book regarding a disability. In the case of young children, read aloud to the child or have the child read aloud to you if they are able. When the book reading time is over, it is appropriate to generate questions about what has been read. Encourage the child to talk further about the book by asking, "What did you like about this book? Which character in the story did you like best? Which picture did you like best? What did you think about the way the boy in the book did_____?"

The story below is an example of how books can help children with special needs.

Justin has been diagnosed with ADHD and his physician has recommended taking a medication to help with the disorder. Justin's parents are concerned about how best to approach this medication with Justin. The physician recommends the use of several books that are written for children specifically on this topic. The parent's purchased two books that the physician recommended to them— *Otto Takes His Medicine* (Magination Press, 1995) and *Putting on the Brakes* (Magination Press, 1991). These books deal with the real-life situation of having ADHD that is similar to what Justin is experiencing. Each of these books help the child see in a very simple way why medication is used to treat ADHD and how it works as well as providing other information about this disorder in a story-like way. Justin's parents scheduled a special time when they could read these books with Justin. Justin enjoyed the books, and the experience provided the opportunity, in a very easy way, to introduce concepts of ADHD, medication, and other information to him. Children often feel relief and acceptance when they read a book that realistically portrays a situation similar to their own. In fact Justin's comment throughout the reading was "That boy is just like me!" In this positive way, the book serves as a tool, carrying a message to the reader that they are "okay!" After the book was finished, Justin's parents talked with him at length. They told him they were going to ask him to take the medication like the boy in the story but that he would have to still work very hard. They wanted Justin to know it was his hard efforts working with the medicine that would make a difference, not just the medication alone. The books also offered some personal support strategies that parents could relate to and model from later as Justin continued on the therapeutic plan .

Books dealing with a variety of disabling conditions are available through local bookstores and libraries. Contact your local children's librarian for suggested titles. In addition, many support groups may also have a resource list for these types of books. Another source for selecting books is the Internet. You can seek books by title, author or subject on the Internet. See the Resource chapter for companies that sell books of this type.

Once you decide on a book, share it first with the child's parent, being sure the material contained in the book are areas of information they want their child to know. You will always want to ask permission to read it to your grandchild. If there is any doubt about the use of the book, do not share it at this time. Simply store and it and tell the family it is available for them when they would like to use it. Here is a list of several books that can be used for bibliotherapy activities.

Attention Deficit Hyperactivity Disorder
Corman, C. & Trevino, E. (1995). *Eukee the jumpy, jumpy, elephant.* Rockville, MD: Woodbine House.

Galvin, M. (1992). *Otto learns about his medicine: A story about medication for hyperactive children.* New York: Imagination Press.

Gordon, M. (1991). *Jumping Johnny: Get back to work!* DeWitt, NY: GSI Publications.

Lotz, K. (1993). *Can't sit still.* New York: Dutton Children's Books.

Levine, M. (1992). *All kinds of minds.* Cambridge, MA: Educators Publishing Service.

Moss, D. (1989). *Shelley, the hyperactive turtle.* Rockville, MD. Woodbine House.

Nadeau, K. & Dixson, E. (1997). *Learning to slow down and pay attention.* New York: Brunner-Mazel.

Roberts, B. (1998) *Phoebe Flower's adventures.* Bethesda, MD. Advantage Books.

Quinn, P. (1991). *Putting on the brakes.* New York: Brunner-Mazel.

94

Cerebral Palsy and Physical Handicaps
Gould, M. (1982). *Golden daffodils.*Reading, MA: Addison-Wesley.
Rabe, F. (1981). *The balancing girl.* New York: Dutton.
Rosenburg, M. (1983). *My friend Leslie: The story of a handicapped child.* New York: Lothrop.
Stein, S. (1974). *About handicaps: An open family book for parents and children together.* New York: Walker.
White, P. (1978). *Janet at school.* New York: Harper & Row.

Learning Disabilities
Freidberg, J. (1985). *Accept me as I am.* New York: Bowker.
Haynes, H. (1980). *Square head and me.* Philadelphia: Westminster Press.
Horman, B. (1986). *Learning my way. I'm a winner.* Minneapolis: Dillion Press.
Lasker, J. (1974). *He's my brother.* Chicago: Whitman Books.
Pevsner, S. (1977). *Keep stompin till the music stops.* New York: Seabury Press.

Grandparent Relationships
Munsch, R. (1986). *Love you forever.* Ontario, Canada: Firefly Books.
Silverstein, S. (1964). *The giving tree.* New York: Harper & Row.

Hearing Impaired
Arthur, C. (1979). *My sister's silent world.* Chicago: Children's Press.
Levine, E. (1974). *Lisa and her soundless world.* New York: Human Science Press.
Peterson, J. (1977). *I have a sister: My sister is deaf.* New York: Harper & Row.
Spradley,T. (1970). *Deaf like me.* New York: Random House.
West, P. (1970). *Words for a deaf daughter.* New York: Harper & Row.

Mental Retardation

Brightman, A. (1976). *Like me.* Boston: Little and Brown.

Clifton, L. (1980). *My friend Jacob.* New York: Dutton.

Fassler, J. (1969). *One little girl.* New York: Human Sciences Press.

Sobol, H. (1970). *My brother Steven is retarded.* New York: Macmillan.

Other Behavior Issues

Shapiro,L. (1993). *Sometimes I drive my mom crazy, but I know she's crazy about me.* King of Prussia, PA: The Center for Applied Psychology.

Spinelli, E.(1991). *Somebody loves you, Mr. Hatch.* New York: Bradbury.

Stevenon,J.(1991).*The worst person's Christmas.* New York: Greenwillow.

Visual Impairments

Keats, E. (1971). *Apartment three.* New York: Macmillan.

Thomas, W. (1980). *The new boy is blind.* New York: Messner.

MacLachlan,P. (1979). *Through grandpa's eyes.* New York: Harper & Row.

Montgomery, E. (1979). *Seeing in the dark.* Champaign, Ill: Garrard.

One company, Gareth Stevens Publications, specializes in books about children with special needs. This company is an outstanding resource for high quality children's books about disabilities. For information call (800) 341-3569.

Bergman, T. (1989). *Going places: Children living with cerebral palsy.* WI: Gareth Stevens Inc.

Bergman, T. (1989). *Finding a common language: Children living with deafness.*WI: Gareth Stevens Inc.

Bergman, T. (1989). *One day at a time: Children living with leukemia.* WI: Gareth Stevens Inc.

Bergman, T. (1989). *Seeing in special ways: Children living with blindness.* WI: Gareth Stevens Inc.

Bergman, T. (1989). *We laugh, we love, we cry: Chldren living with mental retardation.* WI: Gareth Stevens Inc.

Bergman, T. (1989). *On our own terms: Children living with physical disabilities.* WI: Gareth Stevens Inc.

Sibling Rivalry

Relationships in the family are influenced by the personality of each child. In every family, sibling relationships differ. Within a family structure we can witness and note the unique differences in each child. In some families, there is a close companionship between siblings and a sense of loyalty. In other families, there is a competition among siblings for attention and control. When a sibling has a disability it changes the chemistry of the sibling relationships. Children are often very caring and loving to the sibling with the challenge. However, many siblings become over concerned and burdened by the presence of the child with a disability in the family. Often the disabled child receives such attention from the family, be it positive or negative, that the sibling without the disability may feel left out. In one family in my practice, there were two children, one with Down syndrome, one without. The child with Down syndrome was receiving so much attention due to his particular needs that his sibling cried out "I wish I had Down syndrome too, so everyone would be helping me!"

Research indicates that siblings of disabled brothers and sisters may be at risk for having their emotional needs neglected, but they may receive some benefits as well. Siblings of exceptional children often had an increased understanding of other people, more tolerance and compassion and a greater appreciation of good health and intelligence (Grossman, F.,1972).

As a grandparent you can play a supportive role in the family by giving each child a little of your time and not focusing too much time or money on one grandchild. Seek to find the strengths in each child. Carefully monitor your time with each grandchild.

Equally give gifts, cards and even e-mail time to each child. Never speak negatively about siblings in front of one another. Model positive language and demonstrate concern for others less fortunate. Let each grandchild know what it is that is unique about them and the part of their lives that you appreciate and are thankful for. Help your grandchildren see that you are there for each and every one of them.

It is helpful to sit down and talk with the sibling about their special needs brother or sister. Openly discussing the disability helps the sibling feel like they can speak out and talk about their concerns. You may become your grandchild's sounding board about these very sensitive issues. Your job will be to listen. Don't condone expressions of anger and pain that the sibling may share. Much of the emotional support comes just from listening. Some of the concerns that are typical for siblings of disabled youngsters include feelings of anger, worries about who will care for their brother or sister in the future, competition for parents' time and attention and what to tell friends about their sibling. These are just a few of the issues that grandparents can help brothers and sisters discuss. You can help the brothers and sisters to be a part of the family's adaptation to these changes and concerns. The opportunity for grandparents to listen and share in a nonjudgmental atmosphere can lessen the isolation that many siblings of special needs children may experience. The sibling needs to feel that he or she can share feelings of concern and pain. They need to know what they share is confidential. Accept this role with respect and provide your best listening posture.

In the words of Fitzhugh Dobson, M.D., noted parent authority, children need to know that they're loved "uniquely," not "equally." Love cannot be measured and balanced. Sometimes one child's needs are greater than another's at a particular time, but that doesn't mean the child is loved more. Instead, give each child support, love and attention without associating your behavior toward him with your behavior toward another child.

When you are responsible for childcare or when your grandchildren are visiting, prepare for success and attempt to plan ahead to reduce sibling rivalry. Here are some typical situations you might encounter when all the grandchildren come to visit and some suggestions for providing "calm for the conflict."

Old Is Not a Four Letter Word

In today's youth-worshipping society, some adults feel that old age is like being in a foreign country, a place with its own language and culture and restricted membership! Sometimes as an elder you may feel unappreciated and unwanted in today's society. This results in additional feelings of being misunderstood and isolated. Staying connected to the family and re-establishing bonds between the generations at this time is critical. Your involvement and commitment to the family will be a great comfort and joy in your life.

As an aging adult, society may choose to ignore you but only if you let it happen. Do not withdraw from society and family. It is ironic that now as an aging adult you may have someth*ing else* in common with your special needs grandchild. What is the emerging common denominator? The common ground is that you *both at times feel like you are out of the mainstream in America and excluded from society because of your differences*! This can be viewed as a negative "different is lousy" or a positive "you and me against the world!" I urge you to dare to accept the high road! By acknowledging the differences and moving past them, you and your grandchild can learn from one another. From you, your grandchild can learn about resiliency and humor in times of trouble. And your grandchild can teach you about hope, possibilities and looking forward. Look within yourself and see the advantage of your years of wisdom. The person who is encouraging and feels encouraged will perceive life in a more positive manner. The encourager is a more uplifting person to be around. Smile and display your joy at being alive and able to participate in the livelihood of a new generation in your family. Show your acceptance of the challenges of whatever life delivers. Make your life a positive model for all and you will be respected as an enlightened grandparent. This will become the most precious gift you ever give. This is the gift that will go on giving for generations to come. This gift will be known as your true family spirit!

Do's and Don'ts

When you spend time with your special needs grandchild, keep in mind the following do's and don'ts as a brief reminder of all the things discussed in this book. The goal of any grandparent of a special needs child is to help raise each child to be a bright, aware, caring, considerate and confident person with the capacity to take maximum advantage of whatever the world offers despite any personal limitations. Here is a reminder to help you keep those goals in mind and intact.

Do List

- Listen and be available for your grandchild
- Respond to the child promptly and in a favorable way whenever possible
- Communicate with your grandchild, by phone, Internet or in person. Talk to the child and focus on the child's interests
- Stay in close contact with the child's parents and be aware of their needs, concerns and desires for the child
- Learn all you can about the child's disability. Educate yourself
- Accept the changes in life readily. Learn to go with the flow
- Teach your grandchild to problem solve so they can cope and act responsibly in this world
- Model understanding and acceptance through your language Model this for your family and the people in your daily life
- Let go of old myths and misconceptions and allow yourself to be educated by your own children
- Accept the disability but strive hard to learn to cope with it and move forward
- Be aware of the laws and supportive resources for which your special needs grandchild is eligible
- Make your home as safe and accessible as possible for

your grandchild so that he or she can feel comfortable in your home and gain the skills to explore and investigate into the world

- Make memories for your grandchildren so that even when you are no longer a part of their everyday world, they will continue family thoughts and traditions
- Practice unconditional love

Don't List

- Confine your child to limited experiences because of his or her disability
- Allow your grandchild to be over protected or afraid to try things independently
- Force your feelings on to your children about how they should raise your grandchild
- Feel it is necessary to win every argument with your child Try to compromise and negotiate
- Spoil your grandchildren by giving them everything they want and not allowing them to learn how to work and plan for success
- Hesitate to step in when your see the child is being abused physically or emotionally
- Fail to set realistic but firm limits for your grandchild
- Avoid setting up what your own personal needs and priorities are when being asked to care for your grandchild, or provide financial support
- Deny your children the right to select special services for your grandchild because you don't understand why they are needed or how they work
- Fail to recognize that there is a major distinction between punishment and logical consequences
- Interact with your grandchildren in a boastful, disrespectful, selfish manner
- Forget that you are a very special person in this child's life.
- Forget that you are not their parent.

Chapter Seven
Grandparent's Stories

"I didn't pick my grandchildren; they were God's gift to me."
Ester Wallace, grandmother of six.

To prepare for this book, I talked with hundreds of grandparents about their special needs grandchildren. Many grandparents and families have shared personal comments about their own lives with their special needs grandchildren. In this chapter I have attempted to highlight some of those stories in the hope that other grandparents can learn and grow from reading these life experiences. This chapter will highlight some of those personal comments and real life experiences, which provide invaluable insights and human expressions of actual life adventures. In all of the following life stories the names of the families have been changed to protect their confidentiality. May these messages be an invaluable resource for your life.

Meet the Wilsons

Sandy and Bill Wilson are typical of the new baby boomer grandparents. They were grandparents in their late forties and are just now reaching age 54. When their daughter Susan announced that she was pregnant, they greeted the information with apprehension. They felt Susan was too young to start a family and they felt they were too young to be grandparents! When their grandchild was born with Down syndrome the entire family went into "shock" as Sandy describes it. "We thought children with this syndrome were only born to older parents." Bill described his feelings as " hearing that someone close to you died, not that someone was just born." They observed that their daughter and son-in-law felt guilty as if it was their early marriage that caused this birth. Everyone in the family came together that first day in the hospital due to feelings of grief and shock. As they sat almost breathless listening to the doctor explain Down syndrome, Sandy relates the moment when a beautiful mother from the Downs syndrome support group came into the hospital room. This "angel," as Sandy calls her, gave the family immediate comfort by describing her own child and his life. Sandy said, " The woman offered support, hope and some gentle scolding to get us back on track as a family. She challenged us to become the family we wanted to be and could be to support our daughter's family." The woman left a video and reading material and began calling on a regular basis to see how things were going. She actively gave of herself to help the family through an initially difficult time. Sandy admits that everything is not easy but now she and her daughter continue to be helped by families in the Down syndrome support group. Sandy feels closer to her daughter now. The Wilsons chose to help the family by learning all they could about Down syndrome and providing that information to their children. They participate with their children in the Down syndrome support groups, and Sandy regularly volunteers to babysit when the mothers in the group meet for coffee. Last month the Wilsons met with a financial planner to begin setting some money aside for their grandchild's future needs.

An Introduction to Anita

Anita is a bright, well-rounded, single grandmother who has invested her money well and continues to work at a career she loves and is good at. She maintains an apartment in downtown Chicago and admittedly keeps only a one bedroom to avoid having her children visit and stay over. She revels in their independence and hers. She speaks warmly of family and her children's success as adults. She sees herself as an active grandmother who schedules her time wisely to include her two grandchildren. Both her grandchildren live in the suburbs, and she visits them regularly. When her oldest grandson was diagnosed with learning disabilities, Anita provided immediate financial support for the family to cover additional testing in a reputable private practice. She also pays for the tutoring once a week that was recommended by the evaluators.

She openly salutes and praises her children for finding out how to help their child when he struggles and she is supportive of their choices. Anita is the chairperson of her grandson's school's "Grandparent Day," and she donated her old computer to his self-contained resource room. When a museum in Chicago opened a special features section on learning disabilities, she arranged for her grandson to attend with her. They went out to lunch and spent the time together talking openly about the exhibit they just saw. Anita comments, "He will need to be his own advocate and I want to demonstrate that positive choice for him and show him he can be anything he wants to be." Anita represents a grandmother who accepts her grandson's disability in a forthright and healthy manner.

What a gift she brings to her family!

Introducing the Lehighs

The Lehighs are both in their mid-fifties and the parents of three adopted children. When their youngest daughter Kathryn was 20, she became involved with drugs and also became pregnant. Despite their efforts to help Kathryn, she continued to abuse drugs and eventually abuse her own child. When Kathryn was arrested, her three-year-old son, Rocky, was brought to the Lehighs and they began to care for him. Following a brief period in a rehabilitation center Kathryn returned to the family long enough to get her belongings and then leave. The Lehighs have not heard from her since, and it has been more than three years. They have spent considerable time and money looking for her to no avail.

Last year they applied for legal guardianship of their grandson, who is now almost nine. He has lived with them since he was three. Rocky had great difficulties in elementary school when they first took over his care, and teachers there suggested to the Lehighs that they have him tested. They were eager to do so as they have

105

been very involved and concerned with Rocky and wanted to help him. Rocky was diagnosed with ADHD in second grade and started on medication along with a variety of other strategies. The Lehighs took a parenting class to understand ADHD and how to help Rocky. When they heard the information about ADHD, they recognized that the symptoms described were not unlike the things they struggled with their daughter Kathryn. The Lehighs started Rocky on medication when he was seven. They also worked at home with him nightly on academics and behavior modification. Rocky is now a third grader and at the top of his class. The Lehighs participate in his school activities, and Mr. Lehigh is the Cub Scout leader for Rocky's troop. They speak openly with Rocky about his challenges and ordered several books about kids with ADHD to read to Rocky at home. They keep up on the research on ADHD through the Internet and last year Mrs. Lehigh attended a state sponsored conference on attention disorders. Mrs. Lehigh shares "other friends at work tell my husband he should retire early and enjoy his time off. His response is 'not until I have provided all I can for Rocky.'"

Both of the Lehighs maintain that Rocky has brought immeasurable joy to their lives and that the new friends they have made through his school, Cub Scout pack and the ADHD support group (Children and Adults with Attention Deficit Hyperactivity Disorder—CHADD) will be lifelong.

Enter E-mail Eve

Eve's oldest son, Dan, gave her a computer for a birthday gift and spent two weekends teaching her everything he could about it. She has become an e-mail junkie and spends an hour each day chatting with other retired women on the Internet. She also uses the Internet for up–to-date weather news and seeks out information on antiques via a special web site. Her favorite form of Internet communication, however, is her regular e-mail to her grandchildren most of whom live several states away. Eve keeps up with their lives and is involved in bi-weekly chats with them.

Two years ago, Eve's granddaughter in California was diagnosed with autism. Eve admitted to knowing very little about the disorder. She immediately got on the Internet and began to get information, which she readily sent to her son and his family. She started a scrapbook of articles and important names and numbers should they be helpful in the process of learning about the disorder. She calls herself the "communications outpost" on autism. Eve recognized that she could help somewhat long distance with information but wanted to do more. She contacted a local California support group on her own and asked for information regarding services in her granddaughter's area. She communicates by e-mail regularly with the support group and is able to hear about important local happenings. Eve's personal income is limited so she cannot help in any financial way. The e-mail access makes her feel like she is helping and still a part of her grandchild's life and disability despite the distance.

Here's The Lopez Family

Edmund and Carmen Lopez were the proud parents of six children. All of their children but one are married now, and they have four grandchildren. On Sunday, the children who still live in the immediate area, visit their parents' home for a very traditional Sunday meal. It is a wonderful time for sharing and staying involved with their growing family. It was at one of these family gatherings that Susan, the Lopez's oldest daughter, shared that their grandson, Michael, had some difficulties in school. She described Michael as inattentive, impulsive and hyperactive. Edmund Lopez remembers telling Susan , "So what he is all boy—is that wrong?" Carmen also recalls that she suggested to Susan that perhaps she needed to be "firmer" and more "strict" with Michael. Four months later after continued difficulties at school and at home, Susan upon the recommendation of the family doctor, took Michael to a local child diagnostic specialist. The result, which Susan shared with the family, is that Michael has ADHD.

Susan's parents refused to believe such a label could be placed on their beloved grandson. They were angry with her for not disciplining him more and providing a stricter environment. They all spoke in anger, and Susan left the Sunday dinner in tears. Over the next few months, Susan worked hard to understand attention disorders and to do the right thing for her son. She read every book on the subject she could find. She attended parent classes, and she visited her son's classroom on a regular basis. Because of the conflict she felt regarding her parents doubts over her parenting skills, she stopped going to the Sunday gatherings. Susan began to see some success for her efforts but finally decided to add medication to her plan for her son. Once he was on medication, along with the daily strategies Susan utilized, he demonstrated significant success. Other family members who continued to see Susan regularly told her parents of the boy's success. One of Susan's brothers brought a video-tape on attention disorders to a Sunday gathering and had everyone watch it. At the end, he stood and said " I saw my nephew in the boy in this video. I believe in my sister and what she has done for him. We all must open our hearts and recognize we are hurting ourselves when we do not recognize the needs of one of the members of the Lopez family."

Susan's parents were both moved by the video and their son's loving words. That night, Susan's parents went to her home and asked to talk with her personally about their concerns. They visited with their grandson, and he shared recent report cards and daily work. They saw the skills and attention he exhibited, and they saw the way Susan worked with him. They asked Susan to forgive them for their previous statements and ignorance. They asked how they could learn more about attention deficits. Susan gave them another video and some reading materials so they could learn more about the challenges their grandson had. The next Sunday, Susan and her family returned to the weekly family gathering.

The Van-Heusen Family

Katrina Van-Heusen was the first female grandchild born in the Van-Heusen family after nine grandsons. She was greeted like a celebrity and everyone, including her nine cousins, were thrilled with her arrival. Everyone agreed she was just about perfect, and her grandparents began asking her parents for daily updates. At about three months of age, Katrina's mother became worried about the child. She questioned if her quiet demeanor and mellow disposition were just "girl-like" behavior or if it was something else. When one of Katrina's brother's broke a plate on the floor of the kitchen less than a foot from her head and she did not flinch, her mother became alarmed. A pediatric audiologist was consulted and the family found out that Katrina was indeed severely hearing impaired.

The physician suggested an early intervention program for hearing impaired children, and Katrina's parents began taking her to the program two days a week. They began to research all they could about hearing impairments and started a therapy program at home with Katrina. Katrina's grandparents on both sides became involved. On the paternal side, her grandfather began a family web page so everyone could keep up on her progress. Her maternal grandmother offered support by providing babysitting for the children at home when Katrina had her special class. And her maternal grandfather became a regular chauffeur when appointment times came around. As Katrina aged, the family determined that they would use the total communication approach for Katrina. This decision to use both sign and oral communication skills came after much reading and family discussions. Everyone in the family agreed they wanted Katrina to have the best of both worlds as a hearing impaired child. Her grandparents continue to support Katrina and her parents in many ways. In fact, two of her grandparent's recently signed up for a local community college class in sign language.

Long Distance Love, Grandpa Joe

Joe and Beth Bingham grew up in the same neighborhood in Cleveland, Ohio and went to the same high school. After they were married, they lived on the same street where Beth's parents had lived. They have been married for 31 years and had two sons.

Beth and Joe had secretly hoped their children would live in Cleveland when they grew up but they never anticipated or expressed that to their children. They wanted to encourage them to make life choices that were in their own best interests. As it turned out, their oldest son attended college in the Southwest and moved there when he graduated. He met his wife in Arizona, and they were married seven years ago. They have one son, which was the Bingham's first grandchild. He was born with cerebral palsy and uses a walker. Beth and Joe have been very supportive to their son's family and have provided both financial and emotional support to the family. One special way they have shown support is to pay for additional physical and occupational therapy services beyond what their son's insurance covered. In addition, they made their own home physically accessible for when their grandson visited. Joe flew to Arizona during his vacation time and offered his carpenter skills to helping his son. Together they built a ramp for the house, remodeled several doorways and designed some custom furniture. The Bingham's youngest son lived in Cleveland, married and shortly after was transferred to a job located on the east coast. The youngest son and his wife expect a baby at the end of this year.

Last year, after a long illness Beth passed away. Joe is about five years away from retirement at his job and maintains the family residence. Both sons urged Joe to move in with them or at least move closer to their homes. With all his connections in the Cleveland area, Joe has decided to stay put, at least until he retires. He is taking each day as it comes. Joe believes strongly in family and realizes it is his job to carry on the values and ideas in which he and Beth believed. He wants to be a very active grandfather on both coasts!!! Joe sat down with his sons shortly after Beth's funeral and let them view his financial planning and will. He wanted them to have knowledge of the family expenses and savings. He felt this understanding would give the boys some peace of mind. At that time, Joe expressed to both boys how active he wanted to stay in his grandchildren's lives despite the distance. And he has done just that. Joe sends a weekly letter to his grandson in Arizona with notes and tidbits about his daily life. He questions the boy about his daily activities and sends small tokens such as stamps for his collections, novelty stickers and baseball cards. His signature is always—Long Distance Love, Grandpa Joe. Joe doesn't plan on learning to use the computer yet he may learn it when he retires.

Several months after Beth died, Joe gathered all of the family photographs and placed the pictures of each son in their own book. He then sent the books to each son so they would have their own photos from growing up. With the announcement of the newest grandchild on the way, Joe sat down and made a family tree so the grandchildren would have a record of their family roots. A woman in his office does calligraphy, and she will be making the tree for each child so it can be framed. Joe volunteers once a year at a cerebral palsy fund raiser in Cleveland and takes pride in that effort. Beth initiated the idea and Joe vows that he will continue her mission. For now, Joe spends his vacations with each son, being sure he is fair with his time. He looks ahead to the birth of his new grandchild and to his other grandson's daily achievements.

And Finally, Grandma Denise

Denise has been active in her granddaughter's lives since the minute they were born. She was actively involved throughout the pregnancy and provided transportation for her daughter to the doctor's office on a regular basis. This was her daughter's first pregnancy, and she was expecting triplets. Denise planned to take two weeks off of work to be there for her daughter. Danielle had a premature delivery, and the triplets experienced great difficulty at birth. One triplet died and one triplet experienced a loss of oxygen. As a result, one child had severe hearing loss and the other was diagnosed as mentally retarded at age three.

Denise has been an important model for her daughter as she struggled with the grief of losing one child and the disabilities of the others. Denise made sure her own daughter felt strong and tried to do things that would cheer and comfort her. As for her granddaughters, Denise has gone out of her way to learn all she can about both mental retardation and hearing loss. She called local support groups for information and went to the public library to get books on the subject for her daughter. She regularly attends a church where several hearing-impaired adults are members and has become close friends with them. They have told her about additional services in the community. It was through this connection that Denise found out about an early childhood stimulation program for young hearing-impaired children. She was instrumental in getting this information to her daughter and getting her granddaughter involved in the program. Denise became a volunteer in that program a half a day a month and has learned sign language.

This past fall she went with her daughter and son-in-law to register her granddaughter at the local public school kindergarten. She volunteered to be involved with the school Parent–Teacher organization, and she heads a "Grandparents Day" Committee. Each year the school invites grandparents to visit on National Grandparent Day, and Denise will chair the event this year. Denise is a single mother and has to manage on a tight budget but she is active, healthy and devoted to the joys of grandparenthood. Denise shares that these are the best days of her life now thanks to the love of her two beautiful granddaughters. Denise's parting comment was " the joy our little girls have brought all of us continues to be a comfort and inspiration to me."

These are the stories of grandparents, just like you. They are real life stories of real life families. These grandparents inspire our confidence as they help their families and special needs grandchildren. They have learned to tune into the needs of each of their unique children, and they have learned strategies for handling specific issues of the special needs children. They did it with effort, grace and a little help from a variety of resources. If we can gain anything from these stories, it is the knowledge that these grandparents have learned to love their grandchildren because of who they are, truly unique individuals, unlike any one else. And we are inspired because these grandparents have become an active part of what their grandchildren will become. May you continue in this spirit of this book and may your experience with your special needs grandchildren bring you love, great joy and most of all, hope.

References

Barkley, R., & Mash, E. (1999). *Child psychopathology*. New York: Guilford Press.

Carson, L. (1996). *The essential grandparent: A guide to making a difference*. Deerfield Beach, Florida: Health Communications, Inc.

Cherlin, A., & Furstenberg, F. (1996). Grandparents and Family Crisis, *Generations, 4*.

Comings, D.(1990). *Tourette's syndrome and human behavior*. Duarte, CA: Hope Press.

Ducharme,G. (1999, November). *One candle power*. Mile High Down Syndrome Association, 11.

Editorial staff. (1999, September 12). Second time around. *Arizona Republic*, 1-2.

Gately, E. (1999, November). Baby boomers plan to keep working. *The Tribune*, 2-3.

Glasser,W. (1972). *Reality therapy*. New York: Harper & Row.

Grossman, F. K. (1972) *Brothers and sisters of retarded children: An exploratory study*. Syracuse, NY: Syracuse University Press.

Jacobson, J.W., & Mulich J.A. (Eds.) (1998). *Manual of diagnosis and professional practice in mental retardation*. p.127-136. Washington D.C.: American Psychological Association.

Jefferson, C. (1986). *Disabilities–the language we use. Eye on family health*. Madison, WI: Center for Public Representation.

Jones, C. (1998). *A sourcebook on attention deficit disorder for early childhood professionals and parents. (2ⁿᵈ ed.)* San Antonio, TX: Communication Skill Builders.

Jones, C. (1987). *The effect of oral reading by senior citizens on the oral language and readiness skills of language–delayed prekindergarten children*. Unpublished Doctorate Thesis.

Jones, C. (1986). Bridging the generation gap: Techniques. *Journal for Remedial Education and Counseling*, 2, 182-184.

Jones, C. (1993, May). Bringing young and old together: Intergenerational programs. *Natural Health.*

Jones, C. (1993). *An intergenerational guide: The grandparent read to me program.* Lakewood, OH: Lakewood City Schools.

Jones, C., Searight, H., & Urban M.(Eds). (1999) *A parents' guide to ADHD.* San Antonio, TX: Communication Skill Builders.

Kornhaber, A. (1994). *Grandparent power!* New York: Three Rivers Press.

Lickona, T. (1985). *Raising good children.* New York: Bantam Books.

Meyen, E., & Skrtic, T. (Eds.) (1988). *Exceptional children.* Denver, CO: Love Publishing Co.

Olson, D. H., McCubbin, H. I., Barnes, H., Larsen, A., Muxen, M., & Wilson, M. (1983). *Families: What makes them work.* Beverly Hills, CA:Sage.

Shiff, E. (Ed.). (1987). *Experts advise parents: A guide to raising loving, responsible children.* New York: Dell Publishing Co.

Sloan, K. (2000). *The IRC survey of grandparenting.* Applied Gerontology Group of the American Association of Retired Persons. Pennsylvania.

Strom, R. D., & Strom, S. K. (1991). *Becoming a better grandparent.* Newberry Park, CA: Sage Communications.

U.S. Government Printing Office. *1999 census report.* : Washington, D.C.

Wang, H. (1999). *A thirteen-year study on relationships.* Presented on November 13,1999. San Francisco Gerontological Society of American meeting.

Westheimer, R., & Kaplan, S. (1998). *Grandparenthood.* New York, NY: Routledge Publishing.

Resources

Organizations

American Association of Retired Persons (AARP)
Box MM, 601 E. Street NW
Washington, D.C. 20049
(202) 434-2296
(202) 434-2281 (Spanish)
A grandparent resource center is one of their many offerings to senior citizens.

American Occupational Therapy Association
4720 Montgomery Lane
Bethesda, MD 20814
(301) 652-2682
www.aota.org

American Speecch-Language-Hearing Association
10801 Rockville Pike
Rockville, MD 20852
(800) 638-8255
www.asha.org

Association on Higher Education and Disability (AHEAD)
P.O. Box 21192
Columbus, OH 43221-0192
(614) 488-5972

Attention Deficit Disorders Association (ADDA)
P.O. Box 1303
Northbrook, IL 60065
(216) 350-9595
www.adda.org

Autism Society of America
7910 Woodmont Ave., Suite 300
Bethesda, MD 20814
www.autismsociety.org

CHADD
Children and Adults with Attention Deficit/Hyperactivity Disorder
8181 Professional Place
Landover, MD 20785
(800) 233-4050
A support group for adults and children with attention disorders.

Council for Exceptional Children
Eric Clearinghouse on Disabilities and Education
1920 Association Drive
Reston, VA 20191
(800) 328-0272
www.cec.sped.org

Creative Grandparenting Newsletter
100 West 10th Street, Suite 1007
Wilmington, DE 19801
(302) 656-2122
This is a quarterly newsletter that shares ideas and suggestions for mentoring grandchildren. Call for a free introductory issue of their newsletter.

Essential Grandparent RTM
Dr. Lillian Carson
1187 Coast Village Road, Suite 1-316
Montecito, CA 93108-1725
This is a support group for grandparents that uses reading as its key

115

element. Grandparents are encouraged to read to their grandchildren and foster reading projects through this organization.

Family Resource Center on Disabilities
20 E. Jackson Blvd., Room 900
Chicago, IL 60604
(312) 939-3513
A Chicago-based center providing support and information for local families.

Foster Grandparent Program
330 Independence Ave. SW
Washington, D.C. 20201
(202) 606-5000, ext. 199
A resource for grandparents who wish to volunteer and work with foster children.

Generations Together
Dr. Sallie Newman, Director
University Center for Social and
Urban Research
600A Thackery Hall
University of Pittsburgh
Pittsburgh, PA 15260.
(412) 624-5442
A universal center for intergenerational work and research.

Grandloving
by Sue Johnson and Julie Carlson.
Cost is $14.95
(800) 262-1546.
www.grandloving.com.
This wonderful book has hundreds of ideas of activities at a low cost for you and your grandchild.

Grandparents Rights Organization
100 West Long Lake Road, Suite 250
Bloomfield Hills, MI 48304
(248) 646-7191
They provide information on state laws and have a newsletter.

Grey Panthers
P.O. Box 21477
Washington, D. C. 20009
(800) 280-5362
National support group of senior citizens

Helping Grandparent Program
2230 8th Avenue
Seattle, WA 98121
(206) 622-9292
This program provides a core of trained "helping grandparents" who offer mutual support to grandparents of newly diagnosed retarded grandchildren.

International Dyslexia Association
National Headquarters
8600 LaSalle Road
Chester Building, Suite 382
Baltimore, MD 21286-2044
(410) 296-0232
A national support center for persons with dyslexia.

Learning Disability Association of
America
4156 Library Road
Pittsburgh, PA15234
(412) 341-1515
A nationally recognized support group for adults and children with learning disabilities.

National Council on Aging
600 Maryland Ave, SW,
West Wing 100
Washington , D.C. 20201.
(202) 479-1200
A resource for many materials and
information geared to senior citizens.

National Down Syndrome Society
666 Broadway
New York, NY 10012
(212) 460-9330.
This group provides current information on children with Down syndrome
and mental retardation. They have a
newsletter and website.

National Information center for
Children and Youth with Disabilities
(NICHY)
P.O. Box 1492
Washington, D.C. 20013-1492
(800) 695-0285
www.nichcy.org

National Storytelling Association
P.O. Box 309
Jonesborough, TN 37659
(800)-525-4514
For grandparents who want to learn
story telling techniques.

On Lok Senior Health Service
and WuYee Children's Services
San Francisco, CA
(415) 292-8888
This center promotes Chinese
intergenerational activities.

Raising Arizona Children
(formerly called Pilot Parents)
2005 North Central, Suite 100
Phoenix, AZ 85004
(602) 271-4012

This is a support group for families
with children with disabilities of all
types. It provides newsletters,
advocates, workshop training and
support groups.

Recordings for the Blind and
Dyslexic
20 Roszel Road
Princeton, NJ 08540
(800) 221-4792

The Federation for Children with
Special Needs
312 Stuart Street
Boston, MA 02116
(617) 482-2915
An excellent resource center with
materials, national information
regarding support groups and
newsletters.

The Foundation for Grandparenting
108 Farnham Road
Ojai, CA 93023
www.grandparenting.org
A group that supplies information on
state laws.

The Intergenerational Program
National Office on Aging
Washington, D.C.
Resources for senior citizens
regarding intergenerational programs
throughout the U.S.A.

The National Coalition of Grandparents
137 Larkin Street
Madison, WI 53705
(608) 238-8751
This group has information on state
laws and an attorney referral list.

The National Grandparent Information Center
Social Outreach and Support Center
601 E Street NW
Washington, D.C. 20049
(202) 434-2296
A national resource center with information about critical issues facing grandparents in the United States.

Today's Young Grandparents Club
Sunie Levein, Director
P.O. Box 11143
Shawnee Mission, KS 66207
(800) 243-5201
This club offers resource informatin from planning family reunions tohelping out when parents divorce. They also offer a bimonthly newsletter for members.

Tourette's Syndrome Association
4240 Bell Blvd.
Bayside, NY 11361
(718) 224-2999

Resources for Books and Videos for Special Needs Children

A.D.D. WareHouse
300 N. W. 70th Ave., Suite 102
Plantation, Florida 33317
(800) 233-9273 • (954) 792-8100
www.addwarehouse.com

American Guidance Service
4201 Woodland Road
Circle Pines, MN 55014
(800) 328-2560
www.agsnet.com

Boys Town Press
14100 Crawford Street
Boys Town, NE 68010
(800) 282-6657
www.ffbh.boystown.org

Childswork/Childsplay
135 Dupont St.
P.O. Box 760
Plainview, NY 11803-0760
(800) 962-1141
www.childswork.com

Educational Resource Specialists
P.O. Box 19207
San Diego, CA 92159
(800) 682-3528

Franklin Electronic Publishers Inc.
One Franklin Plaza
Burlington, NJ 08016
(800) 525-9673

Free Spirit Publishing
400 First Ave. North, Suite 616
Minneapolis, MN 55401
(800) 735-7323
www.freespirit.com

Gareth Stevens Publishing Co.
330 W. Olive
Milwaukee, WI 53212
(800) 433-0942

Gordon Systems, Inc.
P.O. Box 746
DeWitt, N.Y. 13214
(315) 446-4849

Guilford Publications
72 Spring St.
New York, New York 10012
(800) 365-7006
www.guilford.com

Hawthorne Educational Services
800 Gray Oak Drive
Columbia, MO 65201
(800) 542-1673

Neurology, Learning and Behavior Center
230 500 East, Suite 100
Salt Lake City, UT 84102
(801) 532-1484

PCI Educational Publishing
12029 Warfield
San Antonio, TX 78216
(800) 594-4263
www.pcicatalog.com

Prentice Hall/Center for Applied Research in Education
200 Old Tappan Road
Old Tappan, NJ 07675
(800) 922-0579

Sopris West
P.O. Box 1809
Longmont, CO 80502-1809
(800) 547-6747
www.sopriswest.com

Websites

www.apple.com/disability/
This site was created by Apple® computer with many resources for persons with learning disabilities.

www.aarp.org/gic.html
The website for the American Association of Retired Persons.

www.chadd.org.com.
A website for information regarding children and adults with attention disorders.

www.clarejones.com
You can reach the author of this book directly and pose your own personal questions at this site.

www.grandloving.com.
The website from the authors of the popular book of the same name.

www.grandsplace.com
This website is just for grandparents who are raising children they did not give birth to.

www.grandparenting.org.
The web site of The Foundation for Grandparenting in California.

www. Uwex.edu/ces/gprg/article.html
Data and information regarding grandparents acting as parents, presented at national satellite videoconferences. The conference was "Grandparents Raising Grandchildren: Implications for Professionals and Agencies.

www.ldanatl.org
This is the website for the National Learning Disability Association.

www.seniorhousing.net
Thinking of moving closer to your grandkids? This site is a guide to more than 30,000 retirement communities, including independent living, assisted living and nursing homes in 1,500 cities across the U.S.

www.yci@naeyc.org
Website for international communication and information exchange opportunities on issues of early childhood education.

119

Index